Volume XI, Number 3

Significant Issues Series

The Mexican Labor Machine: Power, Politics, and Patronage

by George W. Grayson

foreword by Charles S. Robb

The Center for Strategic
and International Studies
Washington, D.C.

Library of Congress Cataloging-in-Publication Data

Grayson, George W., 1938-
  The Mexican labor machine / by George W. Grayson

  (Significant issues series, ISSN 0736-7136 ; v. 11, no. 3)
  Bibliography: p.
  ISBN 0-89206-131-6

    1. Trade-unions—Mexico—Political activity—History—20th
century.   2. Mexico—Politics and government—20th century.   3. Labor
and laboring classes—Mexico—History—20th
century.   I. Title.   II. Series.
    HD6533.5.G73   1989   322'.3'0972—dc19   88-39000
                                                                CIP

Contents

List of Figures and List of Tables   iv

About the Author   v

Foreword *by Charles S. Robb*   vii

Preface   ix

1. An Overview of the Labor Movement   1
    Labor's View of Salinas   1
    Labor's Prospects   3
    Focus on Union History   10

2. The CTM: The Leading Labor Federation   12
    The Origins of the CTM (1928–1951)   12
    Organizational Structure   16
    The Secretary-General   19

3. Other Mexican Labor Federations   24
    FSTSE   24
    CROC   25
    CROM   28
    CTC   30
    COR   31
    CGT   33
    CRT   33
    Independent Unions   33

4. Umbrella Organizations   43
    Precursors   43
    Congress of Labor (CT)   44

5. Labor and the Revolutionary Family   49
    Government's Political Aid   49
    Economic Subsidies   51

Social Benefits   53
Legal Privileges   55
CTM Services to the State   58
The Asymmetrical Relationship   61

6. Looking toward the Future   64

Notes   76

Glossary of Worker Organizations and Political Parties   81

List of Figures
Organizational Structures of Selected Unions

1. The Confederation of Mexican Workers (CTM)   17
2. The Federation of Unions of Workers in the Service
   of the State (FSTSE)   26
3. The Revolutionary Confederation of Workers and
   Peasants (CROC)   27
4. The Regional Confederation of Mexican Workers (CROM)   29
5. The Revolutionary Workers' Confederation (COR)   32
6. The General Confederation of Workers (CGT)   34
7. The Revolutionary Confederation of Workers (CRT)   35
8. The Congress of Labor (CT)   47

List of Tables

1. Membership of Mexican Labor Organizations   16
2. Generational Groupings within the CTM   22
3. Presidents of the Congress of Labor (CT), 1966-Present   46
4. Labor's Representation in the Chamber of Deputies,
   1964-1988   52
5. Age Distribution of CTM Union Leaders   53
6. Strike Activity in Mexico, 1982-1988   59

About the Author

George W. Grayson is the Class of 1938 Professor of Government at the College of William and Mary in Williamsburg, Virginia. His writings include *The Politics of Mexican Oil* (Pittsburgh: University of Pittsburgh Press, 1980), *The United States and Mexico: Patterns of Influence* (New York: Praeger, 1984), *Oil and Mexican Foreign Policy* (Pittsburgh: University of Pittsburgh Press, 1988), and *Prospects for Mexico* (Washington, D.C.: Foreign Service Institute, U.S. Department of State, 1988). His articles have appeared in *Foreign Policy*, *Orbis*, the *Washington Post*, the *Wall Street Journal*, the *Los Angeles Times*, and the *Christian Science Monitor*. He has served as a member of the state legislature of Virginia since 1974.

Foreword

Less than two months before the inauguration of George Bush, Carlos Salinas de Gortari donned the red, white, and green presidential sash in Mexico City. Thus, the stage was set for the two new chief executives to confront a series of questions crucial to the security of nations that share a 2,000-mile-long frontier, the world's longest border between a developed and a developing country. Debt, trade, investment, energy, immigration, narcotics, environmental quality—these are among the issues that intertwine U.S.-Mexican relations.

A decade ago, Mexico was the envy of much of a world floundering in recession. In large measure due to enormous oil reserves, its leaders promised an economic miracle. As the director general of *Petróleos Mexicanos* (Pemex), the state oil monopoly, put it, "For the first time in its history Mexico enjoys sufficient wealth to make possible not only the resolution of economic problems facing the country, but also the creation of a new, permanently prosperous country, a rich country where the right to work will be a reality."

Such optimistic rhetoric diverted attention from the beginnings of "petrolization"—a neologism connoting an overheated economy fueled by oil revenues, an overvalued currency, mounting dependence on external credits to import escalating amounts of food, capital, and luxury goods (which rose from $6 billion in 1977 to $23 billion in 1981), a stagnant agricultural sector, and, above all—staggering budget deficits.

In great measure, Mexico could live beyond its means as long as petroleum prices continued to soar. The shift from a seller's market to one favoring buyers in the spring of 1981, however, began a slide (later a nosedive) in Pemex's export earnings. By the time that Miguel de la Madrid Hurtado (1982–1988), Salinas's predecessor in the presidential palace, took office, it was clear that the country's energy-focused development policy would produce economic stagnation and foster social discontent.

As a result, de la Madrid—with his Programming and Budget Secretary Salinas's advice—devised a new export-led strategy keyed on reducing protectionist trade barriers, slashing subsidies, selling off hundreds of publicly owed firms, and curbing the state's

overbearing presence in the country's sluggish economy that stag-
gers under a $105 billion foreign debt. In short, de la Madrid
launched an ambitious policy to restructure Mexico's economy, a
policy that Salinas is striving to broaden.

The cooperation of organized labor, which represents a formidable sector within the governing Institutional Revolutionary
Party (PRI), is essential to implementing the structural changes
contemplated by Salinas and his advisers. Led by 89-year-old
Fidel Velázquez Sánchez, the Confederation of Mexican Workers
has long backed the PRI and its president. They have done so even
when their policies may have conflicted with the interests of
working people. Yet, times have changed from when a handful of
powerful leaders could manipulate the 9.5 million workers who
belong to the unions. Discontent spreads through the rank-and-file
workers, whose purchasing power has plummeted in recent years.
Also unsettling is the emphasis on supply-and-demand forces,
which threaten the sweetheart relations that many unions have
forged with private and public companies. The mid-January 1989
arrest on criminal charges of the immensely powerful chieftain of
the Oil Workers' Union and 50 of his colleagues complicated this
issue further.

Unfortunately, those in the United States know precious little
about Mexican trade unionism, important as it is to understanding
Mexican politics. This monograph by George W. Grayson, a distin-
guished professor at the College of William and Mary and a preem-
inent scholar on Mexico, helps fill a conspicuous void about a
movement whose support—or, at the very least, acquiescence—is
a vital component to the success of Salinas's proposed changes
that represents hope for Mexico to successfully turn to the path of
development. In a carefully organized, thoroughly researched
study, Grayson explores the history of the labor movement, analyzes its major components, describes its symbiotic ties to the
"revolutionary family," and discusses its prospects in a troubled
and rapidly evolving political system. Both Professor Grayson and
the Center for Strategic and International Studies are to be com-
mended for producing a monograph that furnishes valuable
insights into the politics of a neighboring country whose future
well-being and friendship remain of the utmost importance to the
United States as we look to the twenty-first century.

Charles S. Robb
United States Senator

Preface

Mexico is undergoing political and social changes of historic pro-
portions. The institutions and social forces that sustained the
Mexican polity for 60 years are in flux. The Mexican labor movement, long a crucial constituency of the political system, has not
escaped the winds of change. In spite of labor's central role as a
pillar of support for the Mexican regime, little is known or written
about it. We are grateful to George Grayson, who has produced
this concise update of the rarely studied, but increasingly important, Mexican labor movement.

The Mexico Monograph Series, part of the CSIS Mexico Project, has been designed to redress gaps in the state of our knowledge and research about Mexico and bilateral relations. Up-to-date
information and solid analysis is of vital importance as Mexico
rises as a priority on the U.S. foreign policy agenda. The CSIS
Mexico Project is committed to providing the scholarly, business,
and policy communities with informed and realistic analysis
regarding Mexico and U.S.-Mexico relations.

We are grateful to the following institutions for their support,
which made this volume possible: Amon G. Carter Foundation,
Donner Foundation, Jonsson Foundation, William and Flora Hew-
lett Foundation, and the Brown Foundation. We must also give a
special thank you to Senator Chuck Robb (D-Virginia).

M. Delal Baer
Director and Fellow
CSIS Mexico Project

An Overview of the Labor Movement

Labor's View of Salinas

Governor Abelardo Carrillo Zavala, a labor leader from the southern state of Campeche, came prepared for the October 4, 1987 *destape* or "unveiling" of the candidate of the Institutional Revolutionary Party (PRI) for the mid-1988 presidential election. At Carrillo's side, but hidden from sight, were six posters—one for each of the designated "pre-candidates" under consideration to become the official party's standard-bearer. When PRI president Jorge de la Vega Domínguez proclaimed the candidacy of Planning and Budget Secretary Carlos Salinas de Gortari, the wily Carrillo quickly shuffled through his cardboard collection before hoisting over his head a placard conveying the ingratiating message: "*Campeche—Siempre Con Tigo Carlitos*" ("Campeche—Always With You Carlitos").

Other leaders of the Confederation of Mexican Workers (CTM) showed less enthusiasm for the party's nominee. In fact, Secretary-General Fidel Velázquez Sánchez, who has headed the CTM since the 1940s, walked out of the announcement ceremony. When asked to explain why he departed early, Don Fidel—as he is known to friends and foes alike—gruffly told a reporter, "because I felt like it." Although President Miguel de la Madrid Hurtado informed this author that Velázquez had proposed Salinas's name in intraparty councils, the 89-year-old Velázquez was known to favor Energy Secretary Alfredo del Mazo González, who developed close ties to him when serving as president of the Banco Obrero a decade before.[1]

Labor's misgivings about Salinas spring from several sources. To begin with, the CTM prefers politicians (*políticos*) to technocrats (*técnicos*). Although the new chief executive showed remarkable acumen in intracabinet manuevering, he had never before run for elective office. And, since earning two masters' degrees from Harvard, he had made his career in Mexico's finan-

1

cial bureaucracy. In addition, Salinas headed the economic cabinet after Jesús Silva Herzog resigned as finance secretary in mid-1985. In this pivotal position, the youthful cabinet officer spearheaded structural reforms and austerity measures that organized labor decried as devastating to the nation in general and to its interests in particular. For example, between 1982 and 1989, the purchasing power of the 30 percent of workers who earn the minimum wage declined by almost 50 percent. A CTM document, issued on September 1, 1987, to coincide with de la Madrid's annual "State of the Nation" address, savagely criticized the government's economic policies. This publication—in excoriating inflation, the increased concentration of wealth, renewed capital flight, and growing indebtedness—warned of the "loss of purchasing power, the contraction of both the internal market and domestic productivity . . . unemployment, emigration, and ever more noticeable symptoms of social disintegration and decomposition."[2]

While Don Fidel evinced misgivings about Salinas's candidacy, Joaquín Hernández Galicia, known as "La Quina," leader of the immensely powerful Oil Workers' Union (SRTPRM) barely concealed his contempt for the PRI nominee. After all, in 1984 Salinas championed a regulation that required bidding for all government contracts. The measure cost the Oil Workers' Union, which previously had been automatically awarded 50 percent of all onshore drilling work, $165 million, as valued by *Petróleos Mexicanos* (Pemex), the state oil monopoly.[3] Even as he begrudgingly pledged his support to Salinas, La Quina (1) assured the future president that he was not the *petroleros'*(oil workers') first choice, (2) publicly chided him for fashioning a belt-tightening program that "impoverished" the people, (3) made a flamboyant show of financial gifts to the CTM and other recipients to demonstrate the union's wealth and power, (4) extended the term for the SRTPRM's secretary-general from three to six years to overlap most of the next sexennial administration or *sexenio*, (5) placed loyalist Senator Salvador Barragán Camacho in the number one union post, and (6) had himself elected alternate secretary-general.[4] These moves, which came in early November 1987, revealed Hernández Galicia's determination to fight any Salinas-inspired modernization of the petroleum sector that might imperil the union's dominance. Moreover, even while going through the motion of backing Salinas, La Quina openly passed the word that the *petroleros* should vote for opposition nominee, Cuauhtémoc Cárdenas, who has organized the dissident Democratic Current within the PRI before his ouster from the official party and subsequent presidential candidacy in behalf of a four-party coalition. Cárdenas ran strongly in most districts that include substantial numbers of oil workers,[5] even though amid protests of fraud Salinas was declared winner of the July 6 election with 50.7 percent of the vote.

La Quina's infidelity to the PRI and its nominee contributed to Salinas's launching a January 1989 blitzkrieg attack on the hugely corrupt leadership of the SRTPRM. Following a police-military armed raid on Hernández Galicia's home, authorities arrested La Quina and 50 other union officials and moved to cleanse a union widely known as the "petroleum sewer" of Mexico.

Its misgivings toward Salinas's government and the putsch against La Quina notwithstanding, with some exceptions organized labor has emerged as the strongest and most dependable component of the revolutionary party, which has triumphed in every presidential and gubernatorial election since its formation in 1929. Workers, the peasantry, and the middle class dominate the three sectors of the corporatist PRI. Nevertheless, despite their vaunted status in Mexico's revolutionary tradition, *campesinos* (peasants) remain at the margin of national affairs. Meanwhile, triple-digit inflation in 1987 that fell to 60 percent in 1988, inadequate job opportunities, and promotion of an ambitious structural reform of the country's statist economy by outgoing President de la Madrid have sharpened alienation among many elements of the middle class. Increasingly, the authoritarian regime depends on Fidel Velázquez and other labor leaders to back PRI candidates, to endorse controversial official initiatives, and to bear the brunt of severe austerity measures as it has in the government/business/labor Economic Solidarity Pact (PSE) of December 1987 that froze wages, prices, and the exchange rate.

Labor's Prospects

The Porfiriato (1876–1911)

A detailed history of the workers' movement in Mexico lies beyond the scope of this study.[6] Nonetheless, an overview of the development of organized labor, emphasizing the postrevolutionary period, is essential to understanding labor's current and prospective role in the nation's political system.

Although worker organizations had sprung up earlier, it was the regime of President Porfirio Díaz (1876-1911) that gave impetus to industrialization and the concomitant formation of labor unions—notably, in the railroad, mining, textile, and tobacco industries. Several factors militated against the success of unions during the *Porfiriato*. To begin with, the organizations that emerged were usually numerically small, ideologically diverse, and geographically dispersed. In addition, conflicting personalities, programs, and strategies impeded unity. Ricardo Flores Magón, who forged the Mexican Liberal Party (PLM) in 1906, advocated liberal ideas before his alliance with the International Workers of the World turned him to anarcho-syndicalism in the wake of the revolution that began in 1910.[7] In his radical appeals to peasants, the lower middle class, and the burgeoning blue-collar labor force, the PLM competed with anarchists, Utopian socialists, Christian Democrats, Communists, mutualists, progovernment reformists, and proponents of other less well-delineated beliefs. "Their [the PLM's] main contribution to the Mexican Revolution, however, was the formulation of the first all-inclusive action program, a lengthy bill of indictment against Díaz."[8]

Most damaging of all to labor organizers was the determination of Díaz and his technocratic advisers, known as *científicos*, to keep peace in the nation's factories, mines, farms, and transportation centers. After all, congruent with their positivist philosophy was the imperative to attract foreign investment that would advance a country whose economic progress had been stunted by political turmoil during a tumultuous first half-century of independence. Díaz anticipated the governing style of Anastasio Somoza García, who—in the mid-twentieth century—claimed to rule with the "three Ps." As expressed by the late Nicaraguan dictator, "*Al amigo, le doy plata; al indiferente, le doy palo; y, al enemigo, le doy plomo.*" ("I reward friends with money, neutrals with beatings, and enemies with bullets.")

Early in his administration, Díaz permitted the establishment of the Large Confederation of Associations of Workers of the Mexican Republic (GCATRM). This national confederation endorsed trade unionism, the establishment of producers' and consumers' cooperatives, and political efforts focused on creating a "working-class republic."[9] By the late 1880s, Díaz would no longer tolerate the kind of opposition and potential "sedition" posed by workers' organizations. Hence, he shut down their newspapers, bribed and persecuted their leaders, and smothered their strikes. Especially ruthless acts of repression terminated violent demonstrations, sparked by abominable working conditions, at the Cananea copper mine in Sonora (1906), the Río Blanco-Orizaba textile mill in Veracruz (1907), and throughout the railroad industry (1907-1908).[10] Police, troops, and—in the case of Cananea—the Mexican army and U.S. "rangers" from Fort Huachuca, Arizona were deployed as strikebreakers when the number and intensity of strikes increased abruptly during the first decade of the twentieth century. Still, these early years revealed a salient characteristic in the work place that persists today—namely, the readiness of an ever more intrusive state to use whatever means necessary, including violence, to quell disruptions by unions and their allies.

The Revolutionary Epoch (1910–1917)

The revolution that exploded in 1910 shattered the ever more tenuous *Pax Porfiriana* and opened the way to a series of cycles in worker activities. Typifying each of these phases was a period of labor advancement followed by an officially administered setback to a movement or leader whose actions were deemed unacceptable. The government was anxious to control and manipulate diverse labor groups through an umbrella organization.

Although the Cananea and Río Blanco confrontations had helped foment unrest, unions were not instrumental in overthrowing Díaz. Yet, his political demise provided opportunities for them to organize and press demands for higher pay and improved conditions in behalf of the nation's 853,350 industrial workers who constituted one-sixth of the labor force. At this time, incredibly dangerous conditions beset the miners who toiled 12 hours a day for three pesos; textile workers earned between 25 centavos and 1.25 pesos for 14 hours of daily work; and men, women, and children labored in textile mills without heat or ventilation.[11] Among the new groups that formed in 1911 were coal miners in Coahuila and printers in Mexico City. Prominent in the urban labor movement were unions representing mechanics, bakers, tailors, bootmakers, musicians, stonecutters, cabinetmakers, bricklayers, carpenters, and other construction workers.

Still, the assertiveness of these groups was tempered by tradition, rural paternalism, and deeply engrained authoritarianism in employer-worker relations. Such traits still manifest themselves in Mexico's trade union movement and dampen the prospect of rank-and-file mutinies even amid harsh belt-tightening. In 1915, when a public transit company partially granted demands for higher pay and improved working conditions, a representative of Mexico City streetcar workers seemed like a Spanish-speaking Uriah Heep when he thanked the general manager in these words: "I am honored in two different ways; in the first place in addressing my humble words to a chief so honorable as you; and in the second place because I come in the name of my comrades to present you our eternal gratitude, because with the increase in wages you have conceded to us thousands of homes will be bettered . . . ."[12] Meanwhile, the geographic isolation of workers complicated the organizing efforts of larger unions representing railroad, electrical, textile, tramway, and mine workers.[13]

The dominant labor force of the revolutionary period was the House of the World's Workers (COM, or Casa), an anarcho-syndicalist organization spawned by Mexico City printing workers in 1911. The weakness of President Francisco Madero, who had catalyzed the ouster of Díaz, emboldened the Casa to assert its claims vigorously, to organize assiduously, and to call strikes when confronted by intractable management. These tactics nurtured its growth and importance. As a result, General Alvaro Obregón, Venustiano Carranza's chief lieutenant, recruited the COM into the "Constitutionalist" struggle. The COM assisted Carranza in battles against both Victoriano Huerta, an officer in the old Díaz army who had seized the presidency following Madero's assassination, and the peasant-based "Conventionalist" forces of Pancho Villa in the north and Emiliano Zapata in the southwest. Contributing six "Red Battalions" to Carranza's coalition enabled the Casa to expand its organizational activities in Constitutionalist-controlled territory. By 1915, it claimed 36 affiliates and more than 80,000 members, the majority of whom lived in the capital.[14]

The marriage between the radical Casa and conservative Carranza proved stormy and brief. Mounting inflation, food shortages, and unemployment boiled over in a series of acrimonious, COM-spearheaded strikes in 1915 and 1916. Alarmed at this unrest, the government disarmed and demobilized the Red Battalions. When Casa leaders called a general strike in August 1916, Carranza imposed martial law, put down the work stoppage, ordered all participants tried by military tribunals, and suppressed the Casa. Worker resistance collapsed in the face of superior government forces, which, by defeating the Casa, delivered a devastating blow to the aspirations of anarcho-syndicalists.[15]

Despite this turn of events, Obregón was loath to alienate workers from the regime. He did want to fashion a new political and economic framework that would both gain labor support and enable him to create an alternative to the militant anarchists.[16] For this reason, he threw his weight behind General Francisco Mújica, a 32-year-old radical who sought to include anticlerical and prolabor provisions in the new Constitution of 1917.[17] Their initiative bore fruit in Articles 123 and 124, which—inter alia—provided for a minimum wage, double compensation for overtime, payment of wages in cash, an eight-hour workday, safe and hygenic working conditions, special protection for women and children in the work place, and compensation for industrial accidents. In addition, the provisions required large-scale industries to construct housing for workers and to furnish schools and hospitals if none were available near the factory, mine, or plantation. The new fundamental law guaranteed workers the right to organize, to strike, and to bring cases before arbitration boards to resolve disputes. Crucial to the settlement of conflicts were local, state, and national boards of conciliation and arbitration (*juntas de conciliación y arbitraje*), composed of one worker, one employer, and one government designee.

The constitution set the guidelines for state-worker relations. The government could use these articles to reward pliable labor organizations whose demands were strictly economic. However, strikes to alter essential power arrangements would be declared unlawful and their perpetrators subjected to repression. The 1917 Constitution presented the boldest expression of labor rights in its era; indeed, Mexican leaders declaim the fact that it preceded the Soviet Union's fundamental law. Further, the document enshrined labor's presence in both the nation's legal system and its revolutionary iconography. Paradoxically, venerating the workingman in rhetoric and legalistic principles has never prevented the manipu-

lation and even suppression of unions when authorities considered such action appropriate to further the regime's interests. The
prominence of anarchists in the Casa and in most unions contributed to labor's vulnerability during and after the revolution. While
underscoring the importance of direct action, sabotage, and the
general strike, the anarchists rejected political action—an ideologically motivated stance that played into the hands of an ever
stronger and more Machiavellian state.

Post-Revolutionary Labor Organizations (1918–1928)

After labor delegates at two congresses failed to create an effective
nationwide organization, a heterogeneous collection of union leaders gathered in Saltillo in early 1918. Convened at Carranza's
instigation by the prolabor governor of Coahuila state, their pur-
pose was to solidify the workers' movement to overcome the
weakness displayed by the Casa in the 1916 general strike. From
this meeting emerged the Regional Confederation of Mexican
Workers (CROM), the first important confederation of the postrevolutionary period. Elected secretary-general of the new organization was Luis Napoleón Morones, an electrical worker and COM
activist who had organized the ill-fated Socialist Workers Party.

CROM's initial anarcho-syndicalist and nonpolitical orienta-
tion soon faded as Morones led the new confederation into an alliance with the government. Morones's close ties to Obregón facilitated the consummation of a CROM-government pact. Obregón
ousted Carranza in 1919, and, following the provisional presidency of another Sonoran, General Adolfo de la Huerta, was
elected president of the republic. The confederation's enthusiastic
support for Obregón in his 1920 electoral campaign—as well as in
his behalf during de la Huerta's abortive 1923 coup—meant that
the CROM-linked Mexican Labor Party (PLM), separate from but
with the same acronym as the Mexican Liberal Party, became the
most significant political entity of the period. The PLM advocated
a "multiple action" strategy that contemplated simultaneous
union, political, and social initiatives.

Several other organizations sprang to life at this time to contest CROM's bid to lead Mexico's workers. The new groups
included the Communist Federation of the National Proletariat
(FCP) in 1919, the Catholic National Confederation of Labor

(CNCT) in 1920, and the anarcho-syndicalist General Confederation of Workers (CGT) in 1921. Bloody confrontations erupted
between the so-called red CGT (whose slogan was "Communist
anarchy and direct action") and the progovernment CROM, especially in the textile zones of Atlixo and Metepec, near Puebla.
"During periods of tension, many workers would take pistols to
work with them, and there were several incidents when rival
groups clashed, or when workers from one mill attacked workers
from a mill belonging to a rival confederation. The army garrison
was constantly called upon to control the disorders."[18]

None of the new confederations experienced the growth and
political favoritism enjoyed by CROM. Although some sources
concluded that its numbers never exceeded 500,000 workers,
CROM reported that its mass membership escalated from 7,000
workers in 1918 to 50,000 in 1920, to 1.5 million in 1925, and to
approximately 2 million in 1928.[19] Equally impressive was the
presence of CROM's PLM in political positions—a harbinger of the
sinecures that the Conferation of Mexican Workers has received
from the PRI during the last 40 years. Morones entered the cabinet of Obregón's handpicked successor, Plutarco Elías Calles, as
secretary of commerce, labor, and industry; in the 1920s Liberal
Party nominees won election to the governorships of six states—
Aguascalientes, Hidalgo, Mexico, Puebla, Querétaro, and Zacatecas; and PLM candidates virtually monopolized labor's delegation
in the national Congress, accounting for 50 of the 52 labor leaders
(96.2 percent) who captured seats in the Chamber of Deputies
between 1922 and 1928 and five of the six labor leaders (83.3
percent) elected to the federal Senate between 1924 and 1930.[20]
CROM was also in the vanguard of creating a permanent union
bureaucracy. As a rule, such officials earned more than the workers they claimed to represent, engineered their own reelections,
and drew on political and business connections to fatten their
bank accounts. Nurturing the confederation's success was the skill
of the egregiously corrupt Morones in both curbing wage demands
and preventing grass roots' militancy. It is little wonder that in
1925 the Mexican president could guarantee labor tranquility if
the Ford Motor Company invested in his country.[21]

Ironically, the spectacular achievements of Morones and his
confederation proved to be their undoing. As the 1928 presidential
election approached, Morones's supporters began to trumpet the

attributes of their powerful and opportunistic leader. His political machinations caused some unions to withdraw from CROM. The number of defections multiplied after Calles backed Obregón's bid to return to the presidency despite the "no reelection" demand that had figured prominently in the anti-Díaz crusade. Soon after his victory, Obregón was assassinated by a Catholic zealot who was infuriated by the anticlericalism of the Sonoran Jacobins. Unsubstantiated allegations that CROM was the "intellectual author" of the murder prompted Calles, who had to manage the succession crisis, to distance himself from Morones, the PLM, and CROM.

The upshot was that a contagion of disaffiliations weakened CROM. The first major organization to defect was the growing Syndicalist Federation of Workers of the Federal District (FSTDF), led by Fidel Velázquez and Fernando Amilpa who had organized the dairy workers in the vicinity of Mexico City. Velázquez, Amilpa, and their three allies (Jesús Yurén, Alfonso Sánchez Madariaga, and Luis Quintero) would later gain renown as the "*cinco lobitos*" ("five little wolves") who formed the core of Mexico's contemporary labor movement.

Meanwhile CROM incurred the wrath of Emilio Portes Gil, the former governor of Tamaulipas whom the Congress—upon Calles's recommendation—named as the first interim president during a six-year period known as the *Maximato*. His attack on CROM "showed how dangerous was the union's dependence on the state, as the very power that the CROM had used to defeat its enemies was now used against it."[22] At first Portes Gil made overtures to the CGT and the FCP, both of which indicated a readiness to cooperate with the government. Nothing materialized from these contacts, but CROM and the recalcitrant Morones drifted further from the mainstream of Mexican politics. This estrangement impelled the state—ever anxious to manipulate workers through a centralizing mechanism—to search for a leader who could replace Morones and an organization to supplant CROM.

Focus on Union History

This monograph focuses on the Mexican union movement, which has played an important role in the nation's politics since unions intensified their activities after the 1910 revolution erupted. Early in the century, leaders espousing different ideologies vied for leadership of the workers' movement. Ultimately, the government intervened to exert significant control over a constellation of unions that emphasized economic, as opposed to political, goals in their relations with a regime with which they boasted a cozy and institutionalized arrangement.

Social tranquility abetted by moderate leaders helped Mexico to achieve an economic miracle as gross domestic product (GDP) increased by an annual average of nearly 6 percent from the end of World War II until the 1980s. As important as organized labor was during these years of robust development, its role is even more critical now as the country suffers from sluggish growth, anemic investment, enormous indebtedness, and widespread joblessness that finds only half of the 26-million-member work force employed full time.

Labor's prospects are clouded, however, by Mexico's adoption of a new export-oriented development strategy keyed to curbing the state's economic activities, opening the nation's heavily protected domestic market to imports, phasing out subsidies, encouraging private enterprise, and stressing supply-and-demand factors. Implementing this liberal model appears essential to regaining sustained growth within the next decade. Until growth resumes, many workers within the extremely diverse labor movement will see their living standards continue to deteriorate as Salinas complements the restructuring begun during de la Madrid's *sexenio* with efforts to democratize his country's Tammany Hall-style political regime. This situation will exacerbate social pressures in a manner that is certain to test the mettle of a geriatric union leadership.

This monograph (1) reviews the evolution of organized labor in Mexico, (2) analyzes the structure and composition of the CTM, (3) describes other labor federations, (4) discusses "umbrella" organizations within the union movement, (5) examines labor's relationship to the so-called revolutionary family composed of the president and the top echelons of the PRI and the bureaucracy, and (6) evaluates the movement's prospects, especially when veteran leader Fidel Velázquez passes from the scene.

2

The CTM: The Leading Labor Federation

The Origins of the CTM (1928–1951)

Fragmentation beset Mexico's labor movement in the early 1930s as four confederations competed for leadership of the nation's workers: (1) CROM, now discredited and at the bottom of President Portes Gil's blacklist; (2) the CGT, which had moderated its program in hopes of winning official favor; (3) the General Confederation of Mexican Workers and Peasants (CGOCM), headed by Vicente Lombardo Toledano and composed of CROM breakaway unions plus the FSTDF, which Fidel Velázquez and his allies dominated; and (4) the unions comprising the pro-Communist Unitary Syndical Confederation of Mexico (CSUM), whose support was most notable in the Mexican Electricians' Union (SME) and in the Union of Railroad Workers of the Mexican Republic (STFRM), the country's first nationwide industrial union.[23]

The divisions and conflicts among workers' organizations following the eclipse of CROM impeded the government's ability to handle labor demands effectively. Such control was particularly desirable at a time of rising unrest catalyzed by the Great Depression. The number of individual grievances filed with government labor boards shot up from 8,529 in 1928, to 20,702 in 1930, to 36,781 in 1932.[24] At first the 1931 Federal Labor Law, which greatly enhanced the state's ability to regulate union activities, inhibited strikes. Nonetheless, soon after Lázaro Cárdenas, who had been a prolabor governor of Michoacán, assumed the presidency in late 1934, an epidemic of work stoppages swept the country.

Calles reflected the apprehension among businessmen when, in mid-1935, he condemned the strikes as a threat to the "economic life of the nation" that constituted "acts of treason."[25] This statement precipitated a confrontation between the chief executive and Calles, who sought to manipulate Cárdenas just as he had prevailed over three figurehead presidents during the 1929-1934

12

Maximato. Led by the Electrical Workers' Union (STERM), most segments of organized labor backed Cárdenas in his bitter showdown with Calles. Their loyalty encouraged the populist chief executive to support the formation of "a single organization of industrial workers that would end the inter-union strife that is equally pernicious to the interests of workers, employers, and the government."[26] In addition to promoting stability, Cárdenas sought to channel peasant and worker energies away from class conflict and toward strengthening the state and advancing economic development.

This statement gave impetus to the formation of the Confederation of Mexican Workers or CTM. Its initial membership included the CGOCM, the CSUM, and the government-inspired National Chamber of Labor (CNT), as well as national industrial unions representing railroad, electrical, petroleum, tramway, sugar, telephone, printing, textile, and mining and metallurgical workers. Many other federations and unions organized at the state and regional level cast their lot with the new confederation. Only CROM, whose leader Morones was banished from the country with his benefactor Calles, and the anarcho-syndicalist CGT declined to affiliate with the ever more influential CTM, which claimed 500,000 members shortly after its founding.

The very structure of the Confederation, whose slogan was "For a Society without Classes," enhanced both the organization's pliancy and dependence on the state. Lombardo Toledano, the CTM's first secretary-general, succeeded in obtaining the election of Fidel Velázquez, a moderate and one of the *cinco lobitos*, to the post of secretary of organization and propaganda. Velázquez won out over Communist union activist Miguel Velasco, who enjoyed the support of many of the powerful industrial unions. Velázquez used his key position to consolidate the strength of the small unions of the CGOCM and geographic-based federations vis-à-vis the larger, more strategically situated industrial unions that represented better-paid workers. Once in office, Velázquez placed his loyalists in pivotal posts, granted official recognition to unions headed by his allies, and—in 1947—employed the principle of one union-one vote to dominate decision making in CTM councils. In 1941 President Manuel Avila Camacho replaced the Marxist Lombardo Toledano as head of the CTM with the moderate Velázquez. Sarcasm and anger suffused the jettisoned leader's departing speech. "I leave this office a rich man," he averred, "rich in the hatred of the bourgeoisie."[27]

Developments in the ruling party combined with Cárdenas's pragmatism to limit further the CTM's power. In 1929 Calles founded the National Revolutionary Party (PNR), precursor to today's PRI. The PNR functioned as a coalition of notables to handle the succession crisis engendered by Obregón's assassination; yet, it evolved into the most important structure after the presidency in modern Mexico—at least until supplanted by the bureaucracy in the late 1970s and early 1980s. In 1938 Cárdenas reorganized the confederal PNR into the corporatist-styled Party of the Mexican Revolution (PRM), which allocated congressional seats and other political posts among four sectors: peasant, labor, popular (middle class), and military. The *campesino* sector, which mixes wage laborers and small land owners, is distinct from the CTM-dominated labor sector, and the increasingly numerous federal workers belonged to the white-collar popular sector. This fragmentation worked against (1) forming a peasant-labor alliance, (2) unifying state and nonstate employees, and (3) *campesinos* and workers adopting an ideology distinct from that of the ruling party. Moreover, individuals automatically became PRM members by virtue of their affiliations with mass organizations such as CTM constituent unions. Federal bureaucrats were an exception to this practice.

At the conclusion of World War II, centrifugal forces again afflicted the labor movement. Early in the war, the government had applied pressure on the unions to curb their wage demands and to cooperate in the "battle of production." Meanwhile, Avila Camacho amended the labor code to authorize the firing of workers who engaged in "illegal" strikes. He also restricted the right of public employees to strike. Meanwhile, the Congress enacted the Law of Social Dissolution, which provided severe penalties for any attempt to "dissolve" Mexican society. The vagueness of this statute, originally passed to thwart fascism, added a potent weapon to the government's legal arsenal. And, in 1942, CTM leaders signed a "workers' solidarity pact" whereby they agreed to resist strikes for the remainder of the war. These actions contributed to a severe fall in workers' income, which resulted in resentment that spilled over in a wave of strikes in 1943 and 1944.

Critics of the *cinco lobitos* castigated the five men's coziness with the government. Nonetheless, the CTM entered the Institutional Revolutionary Party, successor to the PRM, in 1946. When Luis Gómez Z. leader of the pro-Communist Railway Workers' Union, lost his bid for the CTM's secretary-generalship to Fernando Amilpa, candidate of the *cinco lobitos*, he pulled the STFRM out of the confederation to form the Unified Central Body of Workers (CUT). Lombardo Toledano's efforts to create a new leftist party, the Popular Party (PP), prompted his expulsion from the CTM in 1947. Following Lombardo Toledano's removal, Amilpa cleansed the confederation of Communists.

These events gave momentum to the unification of leftist forces, drawn together in the face of persecution. This possibility alarmed the government, which counted on labor, peace, and low wages to accelerate industrialization in the postwar era. Thus, authorities intervened in the STFRM, the nucleus of leftist labor activism, in behalf of an anti-Gómez Z. slate of officers, headed by Jesús Díaz de León, commonly known as *"El Charro"* because of his penchant for gaudy cowboy clothes. This so-called *charrazo* of the railway union in 1948 destroyed the CUT as a rival to the CTM. The action also preceded similar repression of the leadership of the petroleum and telephone workers' unions (1949) and the mining and metal workers' union (1950). "The significance of the *charrazo* lay in the fact of deliberate government intervention to support one union faction against another. By so doing, the government was essentially able to control the major unions directly."[28] As was true 40 years ago, regime-backed strongmen continue to direct Mexico's most powerful labor organizations.

By the early 1950s, the supremacy over the union movement of the moderate, increasingly bureaucratized, state-dominated CTM, again headed by Velázquez who had replaced the heavy-handed Amilpa in 1947, was assured. Lombardo Toledano's Popular Party, formed in 1948 as a political vehicle to advance working-class interests, floundered for want of mass support. Another Lombardo Toledano creation, the opposition General Union of Workers and Peasants of Mexico (UGOCM), which was the PP's political arm, found it difficult to attract affiliates because *charrazos* had eliminated or neutralized leftist leaders in important unions. Expressed simply: the government/ruling party amalgam was the puppeteer; the CTM, its hands; and individual unions and their adherents, its marionettes.

Organizational Structure

The structure of the Confederation of Mexican Workers deserves particular attention because of its critical role in the labor sector and because of its size in comparison to other federations (see table 1).[29] As indicated in figure 1, the National Congress, the National Council, the National Committee, and the National Commission of Justice constitute the CTM's formal governing organs, although the real power—in fact—resides with Secretary-General Fidel Velázquez who has shaped the CTM to advance his concept

Table 1   Membership of Mexican Labor Organizations

Organization	Number of Members
Confederation of Mexican Workers (CTM)	5,000,000
Federation of Unions of Workers in the Service of the State (FSTSE)	1,800,000
Revolutionary Confederation of Workers and Peasants (CROC)	600,000
Regional Confederation of Mexican Workers (CROM)	200,000
National Federation of Independent Unions (FNSI)	200,000
Confederation of Workers and Peasants (CTC)	125,000
United Independent Workers/International Proletarian Movement (UOI/MPI)	100,000
The Revolutionary Workers' Confederation (COR)	50,000
General Confederation of Workers (CGT)	50,000
Authentic Front of Labor (FAT)	30,000
Revolutionary Confederation of Workers (CRT)	25,000
Table of Trade Union Harmony (MCS)	NA
Independent unions, company unions, and other labor organizations	1,300,000
Total	9,480,000

Source: The figures for the confederations are based primarily on U.S. Department of Labor, "Foreign Labor Trends," a report prepared by the U.S. embassy, Mexico City, April 1987 (Mimeo.).

Figure 1   Organizational Structure of the Confederation of Mexican Workers (CTM)

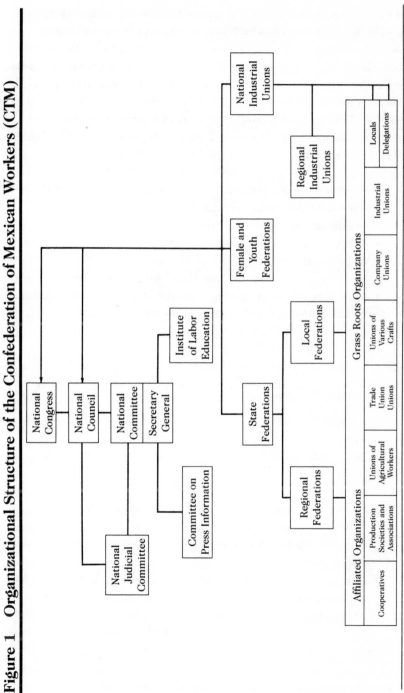

Source: César Zaqueta and Ricardo de la Peña, *La estructura del congreso del trabajo* (Mexico City: Fondo de Cultura Económica, 1984), 148.

of the Mexican revolution. On paper, maximum authority rests in the National Congress, which is composed of three members elected by each of the more than 11,000 unions belonging to the confederation. Unless elected as a delegate, any member of executive committees of local, state, national, and federal district CTM affiliates can participate in the National Congress with a voice but no vote. The same stricture applies to executive committees of industrial unions, the Women's Federation, and the Youth Federation. The functions of the National Congress are fivefold:

- to elect members to the National Committee, as well as three substitute secretaries-general and members of the National Commission of Justice;
- to amend the CTM's constitution;
- to approve the CTM's adhesion or withdrawal from national or international labor organizations;
- to determine the confederation's "*militancia política*"; and
- to resolve disputes arising from the imposition of sanctions by subordinate CTM organs when interested parties seek the congress's involvement.

According to the CTM's statutes, the Velázquez-dominated National Council is the confederation's principal organ between sessions of the National Congress. Composed of three representatives from state and federal district confederations, from national industrial unions, and from both the women's and youth federations, the council holds regular meetings twice a year (February and August) and extraordinary sessions when required. The stated functions of the council are threefold:

- to receive reports presented by the National Committee and other CTM organs and to take appropriate actions in response to these communications;
- to deal with problems presented by entities of the confederation; and
- to hear appeals arising from the imposition of sanctions by subordinate CTM organs.

The National Committee is responsible for running the CTM on a day-to-day basis. Comprising this body is the secretary-general, who is assisted by a dozen other secretaries with responsibility for organization, labor, relations with other entities, political action, education and social communication, finances, economic matters, the social sector, social welfare, supplies, agriculture, and statistics and union advancement. All of the secretaries are chosen for six-year terms; these individuals act as a sounding board and advisory council to Velázquez at whose pleasure they serve.

The Secretary-General

Article 40 of the CTM's constitution assigns multiple responsibilities to the secretary-general, guaranteeing that this will be a czar-like position. Among these functions are the right to
- intervene, as he deems appropriate, in all matters of importance to the confederation;
- serve as the legal and administrative representative of the confederation and its organs;
- convoke and preside over all regular and extraordinary meetings of the National Committee;
- convoke and preside over (with the secretary of organization) all general and extraordinary assemblies of the National Council;
- appoint permanent or ad hoc commissions, as well as individuals who serve as advisers to the confederation;
- make certain that CTM constituent groups fulfill the obligations specified in the confederation's constitution so that they can enjoy fully the rights granted to them;
- admit or reject requests by organizations to join the CTM;
- intervene in interunion conflicts with a view to resolving such disputes; and
- approve the confederation's budget and authorize expenditures in accordance with the budget approved by the National Committee.

The scope of these powers of the CTM's secretary-general have increased over the years, ensuring Velázquez supremacy over the CTM. Enhancing his status even more is the absence of a "no-reelection" proviso in the confederation's constitution. As a result, Don Fidel, first elected in 1941, has served as secretary-general during the *sexenios* of nine presidents, including Salinas. It has been suggested that he has had a longer and more profound impact on Mexico than even Antonio López de Santa Anna, the

mercurial, domineering military chieftain who captured the
nation's presidency nine times between 1833 and 1855.

Unlike the dictatorial Santa Anna, Velázquez relies heavily on
bargaining, persuasion, and compromise to achieve his ends.
While sometimes ruthless in wielding power, Velázquez prefers
negotiated settlements to *diktats*. Indeed, he performs what has
been termed a "gyroscopic" function for the labor sector. Within
the CTM itself, he maintains the alliance between the powerful
industrial unions. Even more of a challenge is preserving the intra-
confederation equilibrium between 40 industrial unions and 34
state and regional federations. Of course, the latter was the base
from which Velázquez rose to prominence and consolidated his
position in the 1940s. The gyroscopic role is also evident in the
Congress of Labor where the CTM, as primus inter pares, forms
the center of gravity. One writer has also noted the CTM's balanc-
ing function in three other areas: between loyalist unions and
those insisting upon their autonomy, between unionized workers
and the majority who remain unorganized, and between discredited leaders and representative leaders.[30]

In addition to the tension between industrial unions and the
geographic-based federations, the CTM exhibits some ideological
diversity despite Velázquez's pragmatism. The most prominent
leftist within the confederation is Arturo Romo Gutiérrez, who
was born in 1942 in Zacatecas, the state that he formerly represented in the Chamber of Deputies (1973-1976) and federal Senate (1982-1988). Romo articulates a strong nationalist, anti-impe-
rialist, pro-Third World philosophy similar to that of President
Luis Echeverría in whose election campaign the young ex-senator
cut his political teeth in 1970. Recipient of a law degree from the
National Autonomous University of Mexico (UNAM), Romo epito-
mizes the new breed of union activist, who obtained their educations in universities and political organizations rather than in factories or on picket lines. As the organization's secretary of education and social communication, Romo is in a position to exert
influence over both the content of CTM publications and curricu-
lum of its hundreds of training seminars. His political star fell in
July 1988 when he was one of five CTM candidates to lose a deputy's seat in Mexico City. The previous year he failed to gain the
PRI's nomination for the governorship of Zacatecas. Also identified with Romo's line are Puebla Senator Angel Aceves, who is

president of the College of Economists, and Porfirio Camarena, secretary-general of the Professional Workers' Union and a candidate, in early 1989, to succeed the aged Filiberto Vigueras Lázaro as head of the strife-torn, defection-ridden Federation of Guerrero Workers (FTG).

Table 2 embraces the generational groupings—those in their 70s and 80s, identified as "*lobitos*" and their contemporaries; those in their 50s and 60s, called "*veteranos*"; and those in their 30s and 40s, called "*muchachos*." Because of Fidel Velázquez's assiduousness in recruiting leaders who share his outlook, age is more salient than ideology in distinguishing among these CTM figures.

Table 2　Generational Groupings within the CTM

Leaders	Year of Birth	Home State	Union Membership	Current CTM Position	Highest Political Post Held
Lobitos and their Contemporaries (aged in their 70s and 80s)					
Alfonso Sánchez Madariaga	1894	Mexico City	Federation of Federal District Workers (FTDF)	Secretary of Relations	Federal Senator (1970–1974)
Fidel Velázquez Sánchez	1900	Mexico	Dairy Workers	Secretary General	Federal Senator (1958–1964)
Blas Chumacero Sánchez	1908	Puebla	Federation of Workers of Puebla (FTP)	First Alternate Secretary General	Federal Senator (1988–1994)
Emilio M. González Parra	1913	Nayarit	Nayarit Workers' Federation (FTN)	Second Alternate Secretary General	Governor of Nayarit (1981–1987); Federal Senator (1988–1994)
Alfonso G. Calderón Velarde	1913	Sinaloa (Born in Chihuahua)	Federation of Workers of Sinaloa (FTS)	Third Alternate Secretary General	Governor of Sinaloa (1975–1980)
Veteranos (aged in their 50s and 60s)					
Leonardo Rodríguez Alcaine	1919	Mexico	Electrical Workers (SUTERM)	Secretary of Organization	Federal Senator (1988–1994)

Juan José Osorio Palacios	1920	Mexico City	Music Workers	Secretary of Finance	Federal Deputy (1988–1991)
Joaquín Hernández Galicia	1922	Tamaulipas	Oil Workers (SRTPRM)	National Council	None (in prison from January 1989)
Netzahualcoyotl de la Vega García	1931	Mexico City	Radio and Television Workers (STIRTSCRM)	Secretary of Economic Affairs	Federal Senator (1988–1994)
José Ramírez Gamero	1938	Durango	Federation of Workers of Durango (FTD)	National Council	Governor of Durango
Muchachos (aged in their 30s and 40s)					
Abelardo Carrillo Zavala	1939	Campeche	Federation of Workers of Campeche (FTC)	National Council	Governor of Campeche (1986–1992)
Arturo Romo Gutiérrez	1942	Zacatecas	Federation of Workers of Zacatecas (FTZ)	Secretary of Education and Social Welfare	Federal Senator (1982–1988)
Francisco Hernández Juárez	1949	Mexico City	Telephone Workers (STRM)	National Council	None

Source: Roderic Ai Camp, *Mexican Political Biographies, 1935–1975* (Tucson, Ariz.: University of Arizona Press, 1976); Presidencia de la República, *Diccionario biográfico del gobierno* (Mexico City: Presidencia de la República, 1984); and Confederación de Trabajadores de México, *Constitución* (Mexico City: CTM, 1986).

3

Other Mexican Labor Federations

FSTSE

Second only in size to the CTM within the Congress of Labor is the Federation of Unions of Workers in the Service of the State (FSTSE).[31] Created in late 1938 as successor to the National Federation of State Workers, the FSTSE embraces 88 unions that represent most of the nation's federal government employees. These civil servants are prohibited from joining any of the nongovernmental confederations such as the CTM. Moreover, under Article 123 of the Constitution, they have individual contracts with their employers in contrast to the collective contracts that permeate labor-management relations in the private sector. Also, in establishing work conditions, public employers are required only "to listen to" employer unions. Comprising 43.9 percent of the federation's membership are 800,000 elementary, high school, and university teachers who belong to the National Union of Educational Workers (SNTE), Mexico's largest union and also the largest in Latin America.

The impressive influence of the FSTSE derives from several factors. It is a large federation, representing almost two million members. Generally speaking, men and women who belong to its constituent unions boast good educations, reasonable pay, impressive fringe benefits, a respected status, and job security. Most of these individuals feel little rapport with blue-collar workers, but identify with Mexico's growing middle class. Their educational credentials and articulate, issue-oriented approach to politics makes many FSTSE members attractive candidates for public offices. Although the federation has members nationwide, its headquarters and largest concentration of unions are in Mexico City, where it constitutes a gold mine of information about the operation of key agencies such as the Ministry of Planning and Budget (SPP). For instance, SPP employees have publicized alleged discrepancies between data collected by the ministry and statistics released by the government on the nation's economic health. The FSTSE is an important component of the CT and also belongs to the PRI's popular sector, thus giving it influence in both the party's labor and white-collar camps.

Despite considerable assets, public-sector unions operate under conditions even more restricive than those restraining their private-sector counterparts. Strictures on the right to strike have made it particularly difficult for FSTSE affiliates to defend themselves against the loss of purchasing power sustained as the de la Madrid government adhered to an austerity program that limited the bureaucracy's size. Consequently workers in several ministries (SPP, Fisheries, Health, and Agriculture and Hydraulic Resources) have publicly criticized the stabilization program, threatened to call strikes, and participated in protest demonstrations. The radicalism of several public-sector unions, for example, those representing workers in the Fisheries, Health, and Agriculture and Hydraulic Resources ministries, is partly a result of their missions and peasant/working class constituencies. Especially threatening to the FSTSE is the de la Madrid-launched privatization drive, which—through sell-offs and closings—reduced the number of state firms from 1,155 to several hundred during the 1982-1988 period.

As is evident in figure 2, the federation's structure is similar to that of other large labor organizations. Nevertheless, unlike the CTM, the FSTSE changes leaders every three years, thereby preventing the emergence of a public-sector Fidel Velázquez. Hence, at the federation's March 1986 triennial congress, Hugo Domenzain replaced German Parra Prado as secretary-general. Domenzain, who won election to the Senate in July 1988, belongs to one of FSTSE's smaller but more active affiliates, the 80,000-member Union of Employees of the Social Security Agency for State Workers (SNTEISSSTE).

CROC

Next in size to the FSTSE is the Revolutionary Confederation of Workers and Peasants (CROC), created in 1952 by the merger of the COCM, CPN, CNT, and CUT. As indicated in figure 3, CROC exhibits an organizational structure similar to the CTM—with a National Congress, National Council, and National Executive Committee constituting its most important organs.[32]

Figure 2   Organizational Structure of the Federation of Unions of Workers in the Service of the State (FSTSE)

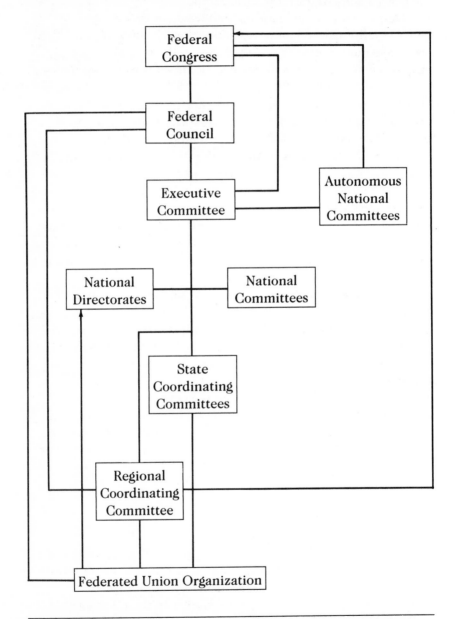

Source: César Zaqueta Ricardo de la Peña, *La estructura del congreso del trabajo* (Mexico City: Fondo de Coltura Económica, 1984), 160.

Figure 3   Organizational Structure of the Revolutionary Confederation of Workers and Peasants (CROC)

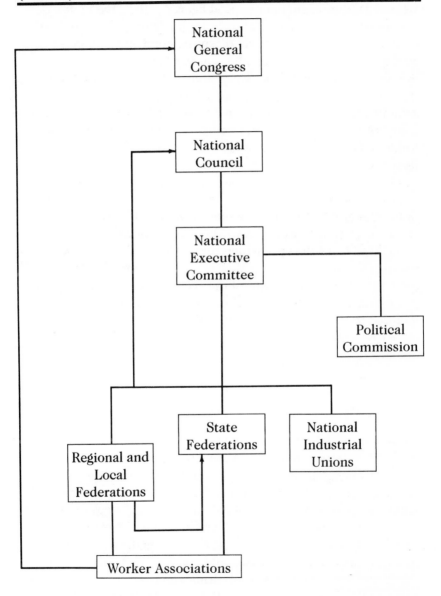

Source: César Zaqueta and Ricardo de la Peña, *La estructura del congreso del trabajo* (Mexico City: Fondo de Cultura Económica, 1984), 151.

CROC boasts federations in all states, with the exception of Colima, Guerrero, and Nayarit. The strongest state federations are those found in Jalisco, Veracruz, Nuevo León, and the state of México. Despite higher announced figures, CROC has approximately 600,000 members, who are found disproportionately in small unions such as those representing hotel and restaurant workers. But CROC's organizing success in such tourist meccas as the swank Hotel Presidente Chapultepec, located near the Los Pinos presidential palace in Mexico City, has led to vicious assaults on its members by armed bands acting in behalf of CTM competitors.[33] One of CROC's constituent organizations is the Union of Garment Workers and Allied Trades of the Mexican Republic (STCRSRM). Even with the STCRSRM's adherence, CROC embraces less than 30 percent of the workers in the textile industry. Its two largest unions are those that represent workers in the General Motors truck assembly plant and in the *Nacional Monte de Piedad* (national pawnshop) in Mexico City.

CROC lacks the strong hierarchical leadership that the CTM boasts. Of course, no one in Mexico's labor movement can compete with Don Fidel in terms of the scope of powers and resources possessed. Further attenuating CROC's strength is the practice, followed for years, of rotating the presidency of the National Executive Committee among the four largest unions within the organization.

CROM

As seen in figure 4, the Regional Confederation of Mexican Workers (CROM) also exhibits a structure analogous to the CTM because a General Convention, Central Committee, and National Council form the key institutions in its pyramidal organization.[34] CROM with approximately 200,000 members, evinces its greatest strength in the textile industry, particularly in the states of Puebla, Tlaxcala, and Veracruz. It also boasts the adherence of unions representing chauffeurs and conductors, the Avon cosmetic industry, and the Aga soft drink company.

CROM's leadership is centralized and disciplined—that is, much nearer the style exhibited in the CTM than in CROC. Indeed, CROM's secretary-general, Ignacio Cuauhtémoc Paleta,

Figure 4   Organizational Structure of the Regional Confederation of Mexican Workers (CROM)

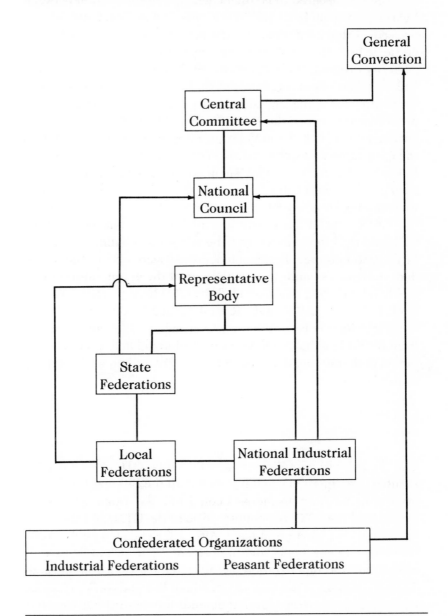

Source: César Zaqueta and Ricardo de la Peña, *La estructura del congreso del trabajo* (Mexico City: Fondo de Cultura Económica, 1984), 153.

was reelected to a three-year term at the confederation's triennial congress in May 1986.

CROM appeared to be the beneficiary of the friction between Velázquez and de la Madrid in the early 1980s. Don Fidel, who preferred other contenders for the presidency over the technocratic de la Madrid, publicly disparaged the new chief executive's austerity program throughout late 1982 and 1983 and even made veiled threats about a general strike. Not only did the president condemn such demagogic statements, but he encouraged a rapprochement between the government and CROM. Relations between de la Madrid and Velázquez improved in June 1984 when the government accepted many points in the CT's "Document of Intention" (with 21 specific demands); the chief executive had used contacts with CROM, however, to make clear that the CTM was not Mexico's only labor organization.[35]

CROC and CROM sought to exploit the tensions between the CTM and the official party over the selection of Salinas as the PRI's 1988 nominee. Both confederations leapt aboard the president-designate's bandwagon with none of the ennui, muttering, and hand-wringing that pervaded the CTM headquarters. With similar alacrity, CROC and CROM defended Mexico State Governor Mario Ramón Beteta when, in November 1988, congressmen from the CTM-affiliated Oil Workers' Union publicly accused Beteta of defrauding the government of $49 million while serving as head of Pemex.

CTC

The Confederation of Workers and Peasants (CTC) formally constituted itself in 1978 when it joined both the PRI and the Congress of Labor. Two brothers—Leonel and Abel Domínguez—established the CTC as a counterpoise to the CTM, and they manipulate it with an iron hand. After all, the CTC's public commitment was "for a new labor movement." Through aggressive recruiting, the confederation has attracted between 100,000 and 125,000 members, the majority of whom live and work in Mexico City's grimy industrial belt that extends into contiguous Mexico state. In contrast to most "establishment" unions, the CTC enjoys a reputation for militantly dealing with management. Consequently, its leaders claim to have obtained better contracts for their members than those negotiated by competing labor groups.

No one has ever accused Mexican union leaders of being a bunch of Little Lord Fauntleroys. Nevertheless, in its readiness to employ strong-arm tactics when vying with either union adversaries or companies, the CTC rivals the SRTPRM and the STFRM, that is, the Oil Workers' Union and the Union of Railroad Workers. Reportedly, the CTC has trained cadres in industrial and union sabotage, marksmanship, karate, street agitation, and coordination of activities with the municipal police. In late 1988, the use by the Domínguez brothers of gangsterism to obtain the collective contract, held by CROC, turned Mexico City's huge Hospital Español into a veritable "battlefield"; the local board of arbitration and conciliation moved its meeting—convened to resolve the CTC-CROC labor dispute—from the hospital to a venue that would be safe from CTC assaults.[36]

Unfortunately, an organizational chart of the CTC is not available. Suffice it to say that its founders run the confederation as a highly centralized, disciplined paramilitary force.

COR

Several smaller confederations deserve but brief mention. The Revolutionary Workers' Confederation (COR), which was formed in 1975 by activists whom the CTM had expelled the year before, has scarcely 50,000 members. One of COR's founders headed the union that organized the Ford plant at La Villa in the eastern section of Mexico City. As a result, he brought his membership into the newly formed confederation. This move alarmed the company, which did not want to negotiate with COR at La Villa and with the CTM unions at two other plants in the capital's northern industrial suburbs. Equally disturbed was Fidel Velázquez, who feared a successful COR breakaway at La Villa might spark a rank-and-file defection from official unions at the other Ford facilities. COR found itself the odd man out when Don Fidel engineered the merger of the three unions at the Ford plant.[37] Consequently, one of COR's few remaining centers of strength is the soft drink industry, especially in the area of Naucalpan. As indicated in figure 5, its structure approximates that of other confederations.

Figure 5   Organizational Structure of the Revolutionary Workers' Confederation (COR)

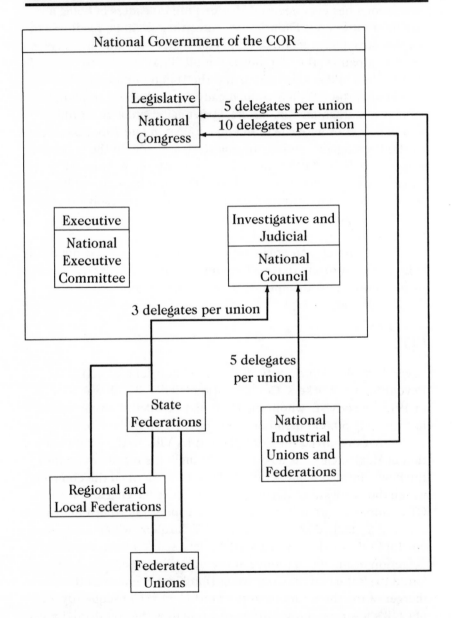

Source: César Zaqueta and Ricardo de la Peña, *La estructura del congreso del trabajo* (Mexico City: Fondo de Cultura Económica, 1984) p. 156.

CGT

The General Confederation of Workers (CGT), which is the nation's oldest existing confederation, also has 50,000 members. A potent force in the years following its founding in 1921 as an alternative to the House of the World's Workers, the anarcho-syndicalist CGT joined the Moscow-oriented Comintern during the 1920s, but dropped its affiliation upon joining the revolutionary party in 1935. The confederation's strength has eroded in recent years. As Frank Brandenburg expressed it:

> From 1935, when the CGT first formally joined forces with government and other trade unions to form a mighty popular force, to the present day, the CGT has found itself in a rather schizophrenic position of preaching a qualified sort of syndico-anarchism while retaining membership in the government's official political party.

The author concluded that the confederation's importance lay in "its ambivalent pleas for an independent labor movement, free of government domination."[38] Cecilio Salas Gálvez is the CGT's secretary-general.

CRT

Even smaller than COR and the CGT is the Revolutionary Confederation of Workers (CRT) whose longtime secretary-general is Mario Suárez. The CRT was formed in 1954 and claims to have 418,000 members organized in 360 unions.[39] This "official" membership figure may be inflated by as much as a factor of 10.

Independent Unions

No overview of the structure of Mexico's labor movement would be complete without a discussion of independent unions. Included in this category are both democratizing or independent tendencies within official unions as well as labor organizations that have staked out an unambiguously independent position.[40] Prominent in the first group of PRI-affiliated unions are elements within the following eight unions:

Figure 6   Organizational Structure of the General Confederation of Workers (CGT)

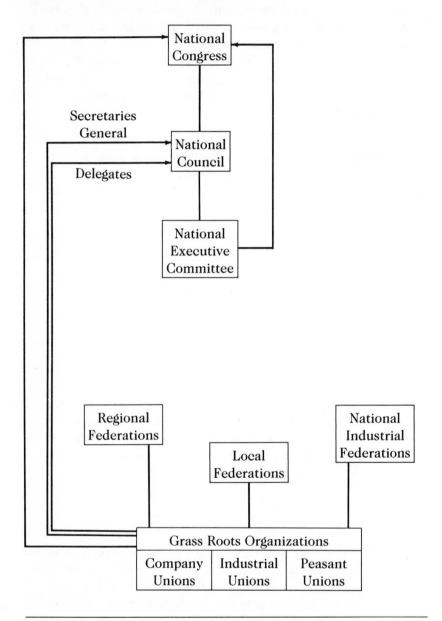

Source: César Zaqueta and Ricardo de la Peña, *La estructura del congreso del trabajo* (Mexico City: Fondo de Cultura Económica, 1984), 155.

Figure 7   Organizational Structure of the Revolutionary Confederation of Workers (CRT)

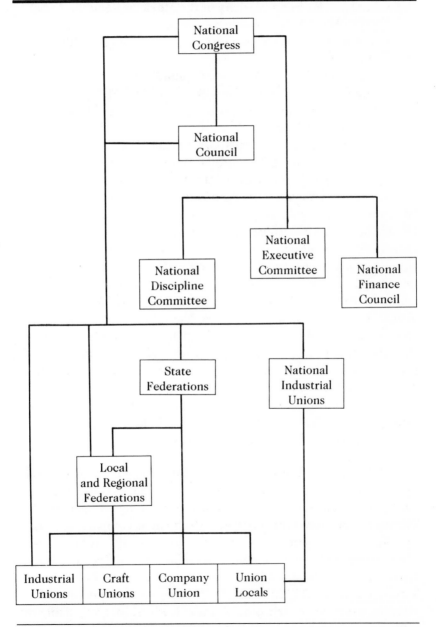

Source: César Zaqueta and Ricardo de la Peña, *La estructura del congreso del trabajo* (Mexico City: Fondo de Cultura Económica, 1984), 158.

- Single Union of Electrical Workers of the Mexican Republic (SUTERM)
- Union of Railroad Workers of the Mexican Republic (STFRM)
- Union of Telephone Workers of the Mexican Republic (STRM)
- Industrial Union of Miners, Metallurgical Workers and Allied Trades of the Mexican Republic (SITMMSRM)
- National Union of Workers of the Secretariat of Health and Welfare (SNTSSA)
- Union of Collective Transport Workers (STSTC)
- National Union of Educational Workers (SNTE) and
- Single Union of Workers of the Nuclear Industry (SUTIN).

Insurgent, independent organizations are as old as Mexico's labor movement itself. Yet, the number of such entities within PRI-affiliated unions proliferated in the 1970s thanks to President Echeverría's encouragement. The 1968 Tlatelolco massacre disclosed the pressures that had built up within the nation's economic and political systems, which were characterized by diminishing opportunities for import substitution, flagging growth, acutely uneven income distribution, blatant corruption, and egregious vote fraud. As part of a broader plan to restore legitimacy to the revolutionary regime, Echeverría, the self-styled "people's president," sought to replace the conservative, often venal *charros* with younger, more tractable leaders who would be less oligarchic in running their unions. Although the president soon realized the futility of his task and extended the olive branch to Don Fidel, leaders of independent factions and organizations had been emboldened to act.

The demands that exceeded all others made by independent unions: increased salaries and benefits for their members and recognition of their unions as legal bargaining agents for collective contracts that were typically held by official or company unions. One key independent leader moved beyond essentially "pocketbook" issues to focus on major political questions. Specifically, Rafael Galván, a former PRI senator and head of the Electrical Workers' Union (STERM), called for ending the corruption and violence practiced by the official union leadership, recognizing the rights of grass roots workers in labor affairs, and increasing employee control over the work process. Above all, Galván and his cohorts endeavored to enlarge the margin of maneuver of the individual unions vis-à-vis the CTM, CROC, and CROM.[41]

Galván viewed the Mexican people as locked in combat with foreign imperialists whose efforts were aided and abetted by a caste of labor bureaucrats notable for their disloyalty to the revolutionary democratic state. What could be done for Mexico in the face of such formidable foes? According to Galván, "The most important [possibility], and the only sane one, is a coalition of the state with the popular forces. . . .The agents of imperialism are aiming their artillery at the nationalized sector right now, and the State can only defend itself if it really gets the support of the workers."[42]

Galván completed his nationalist reformist rhetoric with a call for strikes (even against the Federal Electrical Commission), the organization of the First Day for Union Democracy highlighted by demonstrations in 40 cities sponsored by STERM and left-wing railroad workers and the creation of Struggle Committees for Union Democracy in the unions and the Committee for Popular Insurgency to mobilize peasants and the urban poor.

Such activism horrified Fidel Velázquez and led Escheverría to arrange the merger of STERM with the *oficialista* National Electricians' Union (SNE). Undaunted, Galván organized a Democratic Tendency within the newly recognized Single Union of Electrical Workers of the Mexican Republic (SUTERM). *Charro*-inspired pressure that escalated into violence plagued the Democratic Tendency until its dissolution in November 1977.

By 1976 independents had registered their greatest gains in national industrial unions whose workers boasted sophisticated skills and technical qualifications. In addition to the electrical workers described above, independent and democratizing elements surfaced among the mining and metal workers (SITMMSRM) and the telephone workers (STRM). In the latter, insurgents replaced a corrupt leader with a new secretary-general, Francisco Hernández Juárez, in a fierce battle during the spring and summer of 1976.[43]Hernández Juárez, who was once a Maoist and had also led strikes in the early 1980s, so moderated his behavior by late 1986 that Velázquez backed him for the presidency of the Congress of Labor. Also hospitable to independent activism were the well-paid, well-educated workers in relatively new areas of the economy where there was little previous experi-

ence with union activity. The nuclear workers of SUTIN fell neatly
into this category, as did subway and bank workers in Mexico
City, and the growing network of university professors and
employees, particularly at the National Autonomous University of
Mexico (UNAM) and the state universities of Puebla, Sinaloa,
Guerrero, and Oaxaca. "The labor insurgency seems to have been
a product of the incorporation into the work force of a newer,
younger generation of wage earners, relatively free of the rural
heritage which characterized a large part of the labor force of earlier decades."[44]

Between 1971 and 1976, the SUTERM's Democratic Tendency and the Revolutionary Syndical Movement (MSR) advanced
the most sweeping proposals made by the independents. The demonstrations and marches that they organized were the most
important of the period and, undoubtedly, the most significant
that had occurred since the late 1950s.[45] The SUTERM-Demo-
cratic Tendency and the MSR were instrumental in the formation
of the National Popular Action Front (FNAP), which endeavored to
coordinate independent action among workers, peasants, students, and middle-class elements. Government repression of an
electrical workers strike in 1976 combined with the loss of an
intraunion power struggle led the Democratic Tendency to dissolve itself both to prevent absorption by the SUTERM's progovernment officials and to enable dismissed workers to regain their
jobs. Dissolution of the Democratic Tendency marked the first
step toward the disintegration of FNAP.

Meanwhile, Marxism enjoys its greatest support in SUTIN,
whose secretary-general, Arturo Whaley Martínez, has served as a
deputy of the Communist-dominated Mexican Socialist Party.
Marxists are also active in sectors of the SNTE, especially among
anti-Jongitud renegades, concentrated in Oaxaca and Chiapas,
who have formed the Coordinating Committee of Educational
Workers (CNTE), a dissident caucus of the National Teachers'
Union, and among metal workers, railwaymen, miners, and
employees of UNAM and other universities.

The independent activity within official unions that continues
in the 1980s is a faint shadow of that which took place in the
previous decade. In particular, Arsenio Farell Cubillas, secretary
of labor under de la Madrid whom Salinas reappointed to this post,
has dealt sternly with militants in PRI and non-PRI labor organiza-

tions. When the Mexican Electricians' Union (SME)—a Mexico City-based union—called a strike for February 27, 1987, the federal government acted at once. The authorities "administratively intervened," requisitioned the Mexico City Light and Power Company, and sent in management personnel to operate the capital's highly automated electrical system. In early March, after a week of scattered power outages and blackouts, the Federal Conciliation and Arbitration Board declared the strike "nonexistent," ordered the strikers back to work, and authorized dismissal of union members who failed to comply. Ultimately, the SME obtained through collective bargaining substantial wage increases, which, nonetheless, fell short of the 23 percent extraordinary raise that it was seeking. Similarly, in early April 1987, the government smothered a STRM strike by taking over operations of the state telephone company two hours before the work stoppage was scheduled to begin. Velázquez acquiesced in both moves to halt actions that could have paralyzed vital economic sectors and sparked a contagion of strikes by ever more cynical and disgruntled workers.

There exist several independent organizations that are not members of the Congress of Labor (CT), such as the

- National Federation of Independent Unions (FNSI),
- United Independent Workers/International Proletarian Movement (UOI/MPI),
- Union of Workers at the National Autonomous University of Mexico (STUNAM),
- Single National Union of University Workers (SUNTU),
- Authentic Front of Labor (FAT), and
- Table of Trade Union Harmony (MCS).

Independent unions outside the CT boast a collective membership of some one million members scattered among hundreds of plant-size or company-level entities. These organizations can be categorized as "bread and butter" unions that spurn politics in their quest to improve the salaries and benefits of their members; *sindicatos blancos* or company unions, which are manipulated by management; and Marxist or Trotskyite unions that decry the CT as "bourgeois" and "reactionary" and sedulously preserve their independence and freedom of action.

The FNSI is the largest federation of independent organizations—with approximately 170,000 of its 200,000 dues-paying members concentrated in the Monterrey area. The conservative FNSI assumes an extremely low political profile.

The leftist counterpart to the FSNI is the UOI/MPI, whose 68-year-old "coordinator" Juan Ortega Arenas has been described as "a brilliant, charismatic, but erratic lawyer."[46] SITUAR-100, composed of 10,000 *pesero* or minibus drivers, constitutes the UOI/MPI's largest union. The self-defined "movement" also boasts unions in the aviation, transport, chemical-pharmaceutical, and metallurgical industries—with its greatest influence in Mexico City, Puebla, Pachuca, Cuernavaca, Toluca, Monclova, and Monterrey. Within the UOI/MPI, there is no executive body, but rather a Central Coordinating Committee. Yet, this committee lacks the authority to sign or manage collective contracts, thereby ensuring substantial autonomy for the more than 100 member unions, which embrace more than 100,000 workers. Ortega Arenas describes the UOI/MPI's internal structure as an "organizing base," which performs a coordinating function. As he expressed it, "There are no hierarchies, no controls, no leaders, and the only thing asked of the unions is that they govern through assemblies and that the assemblies make the decisions, not one leader or person."[47] Ortega Arenas, who was expelled from the Communist Party in 1943, now shuns partisan involvement; nonetheless, the UOI/MPI resonates to the philosophy of the Trotskyite Revolutionary Workers' Party (PRT) with which it boasts political ties. The UOI/MPI, which holds its own May Day parade separate from other independent unions, is well known for the marches that it sponsors in Mexico City to protest de la Madrid's austerity program, to condemn U.S. policies in Central America, and to urge a payments moratorium on the nation's mountainous foreign debt. The UOI/MPI claims to be too independent and revolutionary to join forces with other independents. Its detractors contend that "Ortega Arenas was just keeping his workers from mixing with others and from being exposed to their influence."[48]

Christian Democratic ideals inspire FAT, which was founded in the early 1960s when the Social Secretariat of Mexico's Roman Catholic Church spawned a number of social organizations. Originally dedicated to "love" and "the reconciliation of social classes," FAT became radicalized by the attacks and repression that it suffered as a genuinely independent organization committed to improving its members' welfare, first in the León shoe industry and later in the auto plants of central Mexico. Now, it is pledged to "constantly fight against the capitalist systems and union/government alignment in order to end the economic, political and ideological control that the State and the bourgeoisie maintain over the workers."[49] Many of FAT's 20,000 to 30,000 members belong to the National Union of Iron and Steel Workers, the Federation of Autonomous Unions of Guanajuato, the Fisheries Ministry Union, workers at the Nissan plant in Cuernavaca, the Colegio de México, and the Universidad Iberoamericana. Controlled by the so-called Chihuahua Group, including its former secretary-general, Alfredo Domínguez Araujo, FAT maintains "professionals" in Chihuahua, Irapuato, Nuevo León, Monterrey, Saltillo, and Yucatán.

Even though it is not a confederation, the MCS provides a mechanism for coordinating the activities of students, neighborhood groups, victims of the 1985 earthquake, leftist political parties (the Marxist Mexican Socialist Party or PMS and the nationalist Mexican Workers' Party or PMT) with Marxist-oriented labor unions. In the latter category are two CT affiliates: SUTIN nuclear workers) and SUTERM (electrical workers). Other unions that cooperate in the MCS are the anti-Jonguitud CNTE, the Marxist-dominated STUNAM, and SUNTU.

Although STUNAM played an active role in blocking educational reforms at the university in 1987, its goal of preventing greater emphasis on merit, accountability, and academic rigor aroused little interest beyond academia. Thus, the movement, which might have spread across the nation, has yet to forge links with major off-campus organizations. It, like other independent groups, has failed to expand its appeals from narrow, parochial concerns to broader questions of job security and higher pay that might attract a larger following of blue-collar and white-collar workers. Moreover, the government and the CTM have strongly discouraged outsiders from meddling in university affairs. Even so, Cárdenas attracted impressive crowds at UNAM and at other universities during the 1988 campaign. His tactical aloofness from other leftist unions did not prevent Cárdenas's associating with STUNAM and other student groups.

The MCS was organized in 1984 at the behest of the Marxist-oriented Unified Mexican Socialist Party (PSUM) as a mass political protest and mobilization organization. Thus, the MCS —as well as the UOI/MPI with which it seldom cooperates —sponsors

marches and demonstrations in addition to issuing pronounce-
ments on current issues. While the UOI/MPI, however, manages to
mobilize no more than 20,000 for its demonstrations, the well-
financed MCS can attract 75,000 to 100,000 participants to well-
orchestrated protests in downtown Mexico City, as it did in October 1986 to oppose Mexico's paying its foreign debt.[50]

Despite growing grass roots' disenchantment with the official
labor movement and its leaders, democratizing tendencies within
CTM affiliates and independent unions have enjoyed little success,
except during a brief political opening promoted by President
Echeverría. Four factors have impeded insurgent activities: (1) the
personal, programmatic, strategic and ideological cleavages that
have prevented the emergence of a unified opposition to the traditional *charros*; (2) Velázquez's adroitness in co-opting potential
adversaries, as discussed in chapter 4; (3) the vast array of
rewards and punishments—described in chapter 5—that the state
has at its disposal in dealing with organized labor; and (4) the
susceptibility of many ordinary workers, particularly those with
rural backgrounds, to manipulation by forceful, politically influential, and paternalistic leaders. Not surprisingly, younger, better
educated, urbanized workers in modern economic sectors have
surged to the forefront of antiestablishment union activities.

4

Umbrella Organizations

Precursors

Although the CTM's superior position was obvious, the early 1950s found Mexico's labor movement more divided than it had been since early in Cárdenas's *sexenio* (1934-1940). Among the organizations competing with the CTM for members were the UGOMC, CROM, the COCM, the CNT, CUT, the CPN, and the Federation of Workers' Organizations (FAO). In addition, the General Confederation of Workers was riven by three competing elements, each claiming to be the "authentic" CGT.[51]

The government, aware that factionalism militated against its controlling labor, sought to promote unity in the face of this bewildering array of organizations. To this end, in 1952 President Miguel Alemán encouraged the CNT, the COCM, the CPN, and CUT to form a new organization—the Revolutionary Confederation of Workers and Peasants (CROC), which assumed the position of the second largest central labor body. As a politically palatable alternative to the CTM, CROC was welcomed into the revolutionary party.

Although CROC reduced factionalism, the government still strove to create an overarching entity for most of Mexico's diverse labor groups. Such an organization emerged in 1955 with the formation of the Worker Unity Bloc (BUO). Among the groups comprising the BUO were the CTM, CROM, the CGT, the FSTSE, and the railroad, petroleum, textile, electrical, telephone, mining and metallurgical, and social security workers' unions. The government feared a backlash if it attempted to compel the large, national industrial unions to rejoin the CTM, which many of them had left in the 1940s. Nonetheless, the participation of these unions in the CTM-dominated BUO buttressed their alliance with the ruling party and established regime. The BUO was shattered by the government's repression of the labor unrest that was again centered on the Railroad Workers' Union in the late 1950s.

Congress of Labor (CT)

In the mid-1960s President Gustavo Díaz Ordaz encouraged the
creation of still another umbrella organization—namely, the CT.
Like the BUO, the CT facilitated government control of labor by
bringing together a loose grouping of PRI-linked confederations
and national industrial unions—with the number of affiliates
increasing from 26 to 33.[52] Originally, the CT's wide arches
encompassed the CTM, CROC, CROM, the CGT, and the FSTSE,
as well as unions representing textile, airline, sugar cane, oil, railroad, mining-metallurgical, electrical, and telephone workers.
Later, independently oriented groups entered, such as the nuclear
workers of SUTIN. Even though its structure is more sophisticated
than that of the BUO, the Congress of Labor functions primarily as
a coordinating body. No member had to modify its structure or
abandon its bureaucratic interests to enter. The most burdensome
responsibility of affiliation was to dispatch delegates to the CT's
National Assembly, National Council, and Coordinating
Commission.

The CT's actual functions pale in comparison to its extremely
assertive goals. At its founding in 1966, the CT adopted as its
objective "the construction of a new society of workers . . . organized from the centers of power to the organs of the state in behalf
of workers," capable of transforming them into "actors in history."
Consequently, the CT, congruent with its "revolutionary charac-
ter" and status as a "vanguard organization," expressed an intention "to unify Mexican workers," as well as "to struggle in behalf of
the class conflict." It is also a vehicle for "political participation."[53]
Its lofty and assertive goals notwithstanding, the CT serves chiefly
to facilitate state relations with the labor sector by giving coher-
ence to a disparate union movement, by furnishing a formalized
channel of communication with the regime, and by providing an
additional mechanism for state control of workers' organizations.
Through orchestration of its activities with the PRI, the Congress
of Labor helps to bring more than three-quarters of organized
labor into the party's fold.

Several factors limit the CT's effectiveness. First, it has modest funds with which to sustain its activities. Only two sources
provide revenue—90 percent from dues contributed by its constituent organizations according to their membership and 10 percent

from rent collected from various quasi-state agencies that occupy offices in the spacious CT headquarters.

The second factor limiting the CT's effectiveness is that all policy decisions that commit its members to a specific action must be reached by a unanimous vote of its 33 affiliates. Third, increasingly, grass roots workers view the CT as a handmaiden of the government that, in lieu of struggling for the welfare of average union members, apologizes for official actions while cutting deals that benefit a few labor leaders. Finally, as shown in table 3, the presidency of the organization rotates every eight to nine months among the body's confederations and largest industrial and public-sector unions. Consequently, even if a CT president seeks to use his position to criticize government leaders and their policies, his opportunity for independent action is limited by the brevity of his tenure. Custom dictates that the CTM controls the CT's leadership during the last four months of a national president's fifth year in office. It is during this period that the *destape* (unveiling) of PRI's presidential candidate in the next election takes place. By heading the CT in this crucial period, the CTM enhances its involvement in the selection process. In addition, as the CT's president at this important juncture, Fidel Velázquez is in an even better position to welcome most of the labor movement aboard the president-designate's bandwagon.

Finally, Don Fidel dominates the Congress of Labor as if it were his personal fiefdom. For instance, in February 1986, two candidates vied for the post of the body's president in contrast to the consensus that had preceded previous CT elections. One candidate was Hernández Juárez, secretary-general of the left-of-center, militant Union of Telephone Workers of the Mexican Republic (STRM); the other was Rafael Riva Palacio, leader of the small, 14,000-member Independent Union of Workers of INFONAVIT, a state agency for subsidized housing. Wary of the aggressive, outspoken Hernández Juárez, Velázquez and other traditional *charros* threw their support to Riva Palacio, who captured the presidency by a four to one margin. Still, Don Fidel did not want to alienate the energetic but vanquished Hernández Juárez lest he join the ranks of critics of the official labor movement. Thus, the CT created a new position of vice president to which the telephone workers' leader was unanimously elected. During his nine months in this office, the vice president worked closely with his

Table 3   Presidents of the Congress of Labor (CT) 1966–Present

President	Affiliation	Period Served
Antonio Bernal Ternorio	FSTSE	March 15, 1966–November 30, 1966
Fidel Velázquez Sánchez	CTM	December 10, 1966–May 31, 1967
Luis Gómez	railroad workers	June 10, 1967–January 2, 1968
Napoleón Gómez Sada	miners	January 2, 1968–July 2, 1968
Manuel Rivera Anaya	CROC	July 10, 1968–January 17, 1969
Salvador Serrano Ramírez	CROM	January 17, 1969–July 30, 1969
Fidel Velázquez Sánchez	CTM	July 30, 1969–January 31, 1970
Edgar Robledo Santiago	FSTSE	January 31, 1970–July 31, 1970
Francisco Benítez	theatrical workers	August 10, 1970–January 31, 1971
Angel Olivo Solís	COR	February 10, 1971–July 31, 1971
Carlos Olmos Sánchez	SNTE	August 10, 1971–November 30, 1972
Jorge Durán Chávez	film workers	June 10, 1972–January 10, 1973
Mauro Gómez Peralta Damiron	ASPA	January 10, 1973–June 30, 1973
Antonio J. Hernández	CROM	July 10, 1973–January 22, 1974
Salustio Salgado Guzmán	telephone workers	January 22, 1974–July 15, 1974
Cecilio Salas Gálvez	CGT	July 5, 1974–January 3, 1975
Silverio R. Alvarado	CROC	January 3, 1975–August 26, 1975
Fidel Velázquez Sánchez	CTM	August 26, 1975 – March 4, 1976
Armando Victoria Galván	ASPA	March 4, 1976–October 2, 1976
Carlos Jonguitud Barrios	SNTE	October 2, 1976–April 7, 1977
Daniel Espinosa Galindo	FSTSE	December 6, 1976–April 15, 1977
Napoleón Gómez Sada	miners	April 15, 1977–November 4, 1977
Jesús Martínez Gortari	railroad workers	November 4, 1977–May 17, 1978
Oscar Torres Pancardo	oil workers	May 17, 1978–November 17, 1978
Cecilio Salas Gálvez	CGT	February 17, 1979–September 21, 1979
José Luis Andrade Ibarra	SNTE	September 21, 1979–March 21, 1980
Angel Olivo Solís	COR	May 6, 1980–January 12, 1981
Faustino Alba Zavala	railroad workers	January 12, 1981–August 14, 1981
Fidel Velázquez Sánchez	CTM	August 14, 1981–May 24, 1982
Luis José Dorantes Segovia	FSTSE	May 24, 1982–January 28, 1983
Napoleón Gómez Sada	miners	January 28, 1983–October 11, 1983
Homero Flores González	ASPA	October 11, 1983–June 6, 1984
Mateo De Regil Rodríguez	SNTSS	June 6, 1984–January 18, 1985
Angel Olivo Solís	COR	February 18, 1985–February 18, 1986
Rafael Riva Palacio Pontones	INFONAVIT	February 18, 1986–January 18, 1987
Francisco Hernández Juárez	telephone workers	January 19, 1987–July 18, 1987
Fidel Velázquez Sánchez	CTM	July 18, 1987–June 18, 1988*
Jorge Sánchez García	SME	June 18, 1988–

*Velázquez's term was extended because of sensitive negotiations between the labor sector and the government over the Economic Solidarity Pact

Source: *Congreso del Trabajo*, 114 (February 1987): 18; interviews at the CT headquarters.

Figure 8   Organizational Structure of the Congress of Labor (CT)

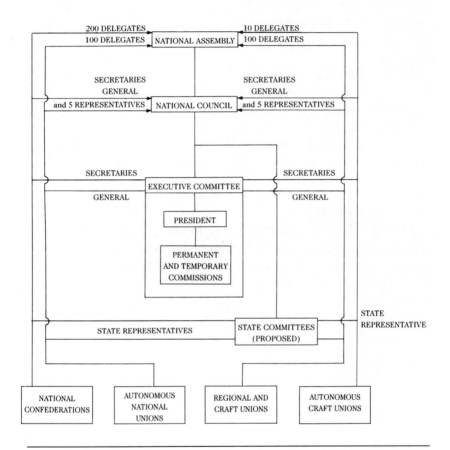

Source: César Zaqueta and Ricardo de la Peña, *La estructura del congreso del trabajo* (Mexico City: Fondo de Cultura Económica, 1984), 111.

president, frequently consulted Velázquez whose advice he followed, and moderated his public statements. Then in December 1986, when Hernández Juárez again sought the CT presidency, he obtained the full backing of Velázquez and was easily elected. As president, the STRM leader proved a paragon of moderation. Evidently, he had learned the maxim "to get along you must go along."

Moreover, politics may have loomed large in the choice of Velázquez's successor as CT president in mid-1988. The selection of Jorge Sánchez García, the militant secretary-general of the Mexican Electricians' Union (SME), may have sprung from a desire to place a firebrand at the CT's helm to exact concessions from a government relying heavily on wage limitation to combat inflation. In any case, the CT furnishes a safety valve for disgruntled union leaders who wish to vent their spleen at the Economic Solidarity Pact (PSE) or other programs. The organization also provides a forum for posturing by Fidel Velázquez and others who support—for instance, the PSE, because it provides a mechanism for labor/business/government negotiations—yet wish to convey the image of relentless struggle against an oppressive economic accord.

5

Labor and the Revolutionary Family

Although the government's relations with the CTM are interdependent, the government is predominant. It assists the CTM through giving political, economic, social, and legal benefits.[54] In return, the CTM provides invaluable services for the state.

The Government's Political Aid

Most important among its political contributions is the government's readiness to use coercive force against challenges either to the CTM and other pro-PRI labor organizations or to incumbent leaders of CTM constituent unions. For instance, from 1948 to 1951, the Alemán regime guaranteed the CTM's dominance in the labor sector by deploying military and police units against opposition groups in key industrial unions and against the Coalition of Worker and Peasant Organizations. And in 1959, President Adolfo López Mateos also resorted to force to terminate the railroad workers' strike, thereby ending "a major mobilizational challenge to the 'official' labor movement represented by the CTM."[55]

The government also helps to suppress intraunion challenges to the *charros* mounted by factions espousing independence, militancy, and democracy. During Echeverría's term from 1970 to 1976, Secretary of Labor Porfirio Muñoz Ledo—who is now a federal senator, was chief adviser to the 1988 opposition presidential candidate, Cuauhtémoc Cárdenas, and is the prime mover in the *Democratic Current*—personally warned Hebraicaz Vázquez Gutiérrez, the leader of a small reformist movement within the powerful Oil Workers' Union (SRTPRM), against continuing his activities. During a meeting in the Ministry of Labor, Muñoz Ledo hit and roughly handled Vázquez in an effort to convince him to sign a memorandum stipulating that no corruption existed in the union. When Vázquez persisted in challenging the *jefe máximo* of the SRTPRM, the redoubtable Joaquín "La Quina" Hernández Galicia, Vázquez was jailed for six months, stripped of the tenured position that he had held for 19 years in Pemex, and blackballed from obtaining employment with other CTM-affiliated unions.[56] In mid-1978, when construction workers at the northern copper mine of La Caridad at Nacozari, precipitated a campaign to form an independent union, the government sent in soldiers and police to quell the strike. In total, more than 100 strikers were arrested and a dozen leaders were charged with damaging installations.[57]

In general the government, which works closely with the official union hierarchy, prefers co-optation to coercion. This technique has been used effectively with the huge strife-ridden teachers' union, the SNTE. Although the conflict between the state as an employer and this key segment of the work force continues (as well as an intra-SNTE struggle), the dissident leadership in several states has been demobilized by elevating them to prestigious and lucrative posts on state committees of the national union.[58] In addition, the Ministry of Labor has turned a blind eye as the SNTE, dreading a strong challenge from anti-Jonguitud dissidents in the rival CNTE, has failed to abide by the union's constitution and hold state conventions in such opposition hotbeds as Oaxaca and Chiapas.

Reportedly, the CTM has its own shock troops who, acting alone or in concert with local authorities, keep internal dissidents in line, challenge competing labor organizations, and bring pressure to bear on uncooperative corporations. According to the weekly *Proceso*, Wallace de la Mancha, a shadowy 56-year-old activist who personally manages a number of labor contracts in Mexico state, has created Fidel Velázquez Sindical Organizations and Gregorio Velázquez Sindical Organizations (named for Don Fidel's older brother who until recently was the labor patriarch of Mexico state). These organizations employ force against CTM adversaries. Apparently, Wallace has recruited scores of young, umemployed men in the Mexico City area to carry out his missions. Such firms as Samsonite, Rassini Rheen, Comercializadora de Industria, and Galvanizadora Nacional have been identified as recent targets of his strong-arm tactics. Participants in the November 1988 CTM-CROC violence at Mexico City's Presidente Chapultepec Hotel have identified Wallace as the prime mover behind that bloody confrontation.[59]

Not only does the government cooperate with the CTM to punish or co-opt the confederation's foes, it rewards leaders of affiliated unions with a variety of positions in such federal agencies as the National Railways and the Mexican Institute of Social Security (IMSS), in state and local governments, and in the national Congress. Although the CTM receives a majority of these sinecures, the progovernment FSTSE, CROC, and CROM also gain access to political posts. In late 1988, CTM stalwarts held the governorships in the states of Campeche and Durango. As indicated in table 4, labor's representation in the Chamber of Deputies has increased in recent years. These seats, especially prized within union circles, are one means to propitiate labor when relatively few economic rewards are available.

Economic Subsidies

The government's economic subsidies are important to organized labor because of extremely low dues collections. Indeed, between 1950 and 1965, the CTM estimated that only 7 to 10 percent of its members fulfilled their financial obligation—even though the dues during the period amounted to less than five pesos.[60]

Constituent unions have helped the CTM to meet its expenses. In fact, the enormously wealthy Oil Workers' Union, whose assets were estimated to be 100,000 million pesos in 1986, helped to finance the confederation's new headquarters in the Plaza de la Revolución and, in November 1987, La Quina made a one-million-peso gift to the CTM in behalf of the STRPRM. Through special contributions, union representatives in Congress have provided additional funds for operations.

Still, unspecified "donations," probably from the government, have become increasingly important to the CTM's financial well-being. In the 1970s, such subsidies may have totaled 500,000 to several million pesos annually.[61] Furthermore, the several hundred staff members in the confederation's national headquarters receive two checks every pay period: one from the CTM, the other from the PRI. The ruling party also transfers money to the confederation when it rents its large auditorium or uses other CTM facilities.

Table 4   Labor's Representation in the Chamber of Deputies, 1964–1988

	Total Number of PRI Deputies	Total Number of Labor Delegates	Labor Delegates as a % of PRI	Total Number of CTM Deputies	CTM Deputies as a % of PRI	CTM Deputies of a % of entire Labor Delegation
1964-1967—XLVI	177	27	15.3	17	9.6	63.0
1967-1970—XLVII	172	34	19.8	14	8.1	41.2
1970-1973—XLVIII	150	25	16.7	14	9.3	56.0
1973-1976—XLIX	173	27	15.6	20	11.6	74.1
1976-1979—L	262	39	14.9	23	8.8	59.0
1979-1982—LI	294	66	22.4	43	14.6	65.2
1982-1985—LII	300	73	24.3	50	16.7	68.5
1985-1988—LIII	289	71	24.6	44	15.2	62.0

Sources: César Zaqueta and Ricardo de la Peña, *La estructura del congreso del trabajo, estado, trabajo y capital en méxico: un acercamiento al tema* (Mexico City: Fondo de Cultura Económica, 1984); Cámara de Diputados, *Directorio: 1982-1985* (Mexico City: Congreso de la Unión, n.d.); and data supplied by Deputy Lic. Fernando Ortiz Arana, Secretary of Electoral Action, PRI.

Table 5   Age Distribution of CTM Union Leaders

Number of Leaders in Each Age Category	State Federations (34)	Industrial Unions (39)
25–29	1	0
30–34	0	2
35–39	1	5
40–44	0	5
45–49	4	6
50–54	8	7
55–59	6	6
60–64	4	7
65–69	3	0
70–74	4	0
75–79	0	0
80–84	3	1

Source: Information provided on a confidential basis by officials of the Confederation of Mexican Workers, 1987.

Social Benefits

Social subsidies guarantee that members of progovernment unions are an elite within Mexico's work force. Foremost among worker benefits are those provided by the IMSS, the Mexican Institute of Social Security. Established in 1943 with a loan of more than 500 million pesos from the Finance Ministry, the institute is governed by a 30-member board or General Assembly composed of 10 presidential appointees, 10 employer representatives, and 10 union-selected delegates. This apportionment brought labor into a permanent institutional relationship with government and the private sector.[62] In 1984, the IMSS provided pensions, medical care, and family planning services to the families of more than 7 million workers (26.8 million people, including dependents), most of whom were in the private sector.[63] The IMSS's success led to the creation of a similar agency for public employees—the Security and Social Services Institute for Government Workers (ISSSTE). Of course, a number of unions—those of the telephone, railroad, and oil workers, for instance—operate their own systems of hospitals and clinics subsidized by the state agency that employs their members.

As a quid pro quo for labor's loyalty to the government in the wake of the 1968 Tlatelolco massacre in which government troops killed several hundred protestors, Echeverría formed a Workers' Housing Institute (INFONAVIT) to help build new housing for union members. Even though beset by corruption, this agency completed 3.17 million low- and medium-cost units between 1972 and 1982. A severe recession notwithstanding, INFONAVIT financed the construction of some 368,595 houses during de la Madrid's *sexenio*.[64] A parallel institution, the National Fund for the Development and Guarantee of Workers' Consumption (FONACOT), assists workers in purchasing furniture, appliances, and other household goods. Four union representatives sit on the 12-member National Minimum Wage Commission, a tripartite body that periodically adjusts the country's minimum wage, which is a benchmark for salary increases throughout the economy.

So numerous are the social, economic, and recreational enterprises operated by the SRTPRM that they constitute a "parallel society" that provides an enormously effective mechanism for controlling both workers and management.[65] In an SRTPRM stronghold such as Poza Rica in oil-rich Veracruz state, a member of the *familia petrolera* may be born in a union-operated health facility, study at a school constructed for the union, obtain a job with Pemex through the head of Local 30, purchase clothing and food in union-owned stores, borrow money from a union-operated credit union, swim in the pool of a union-sponsored recreation center, read a union-published newspaper, and be buried in a funeral home managed by union leaders.

Detractors of SRTPRM's leadership know that the leaders may be putting their lives on the line in operating their own union enforcement agency. Hernández Galicia has mastered the use of the stick as well as the carrot. He and his cohorts readily employ blackmail, inimidation, and violence to maintain their hegemony over the union. Heriberto Vincent Kehoë, the union's extremely adroit secretary-general from Local 30, was assassinated on February 28, 1977 in a killing with many of the trappings of a New York "Little Italy" execution. Ostensibly, Kehoë was in his home base of Poza Rica to observe the progress of a school being built by Local 30. During his visit, he was gunned down in cold blood. Kehoë was reportedly fashioning a base of support among younger workers and those in the rapidly growing southern oil fields in order to supplant La Quina and smash the "petroleum Mafia."[66]

This cradle-to-grave dominance illuminates the patron-client relations that suffuse the labor movement. For instance, a blue-collar worker who seeks something from a state agency—a job, a loan, a house, a birth certificate—may be rebuffed by Mexico's "come back tomorrow" bureaucracy. After all, the worker is poorly educated, inexperienced in negotiating the bureaucratic maze, and lacking in the "school ties" and other social contacts that members of the middle class draw upon in their dealings with functionaries. But the union member knows that the president and other officers of his local have connections with the power brokers. Hence, if the need is great enough, he turns to his union *patrón* for help, which—more than likely—will be forthcoming, provided of course that the *obrero* client reciprocates with unquestioning loyalty to his benefactor. Each exchange reinforces and strengthens this mutual dependence.

In appreciation for Velázquez's cooperation with the implementation of an austerity program, the López Portillo administration turned over control of INFONAVIT to the CTM and established a special financial institution to benefit workers. In addition to offering a conventional array of banking services for individuals and their families, this Banco Obrero makes low-cost loans to both unions and the CTM as well as other confederations. The bank, which the government prudently did not nationalize in 1982, has as its shareholders 88 labor organizations and also finances the CTM's acquisitions of such companies as Bicicletas Condor. These firms form part of the so-called social sector of the economy created by a constitutional amendment in the early 1980s. Among its other operations, the Banco Obrero provides credits to communal farms known as *ejidos*, the social sector's largest component.

Legal Privileges

An extremely complex state structure for handling worker-management relations is helpful to progovernment unions. To enjoy the benefits of the labor code, unions must register with the Ministry of Labor and Social Welfare. Hence, the ministry can reward or punish organizations by either accepting or denying their registration requests. In 1949, for instance, the ministry refused to recognize Lombardo Toledano's newly created General Union of Workers and Peasants of Mexico (UGOCM) because it violated the labor code by including peasant groups. Yet, UGOCM's affinity for anti-PRI activism and its bonds with the Popular Party seemed to have been its most egregious crimes.

Once recognition takes place, the ministry can facilitate a single union's monopoly of a given industry by approving exclusion clauses in its collective bargaining contract. Such clauses recognize only one bargaining agent in an industry and virtually compel all workers covered by the contract to join that union. An even more potent weapon in the hands of union leaders is the separation exclusion clause, which requires an employer to discharge any employee who loses his union membership. By dismissing dissidents from their ranks, heads of locals can prevent rivals from challenging their authority. "In cases in which incumbent leaders successfully manipulate internal union procedures so as to deprive challengers of their union membership, these workers lose their jobs as well. This is a major disincentive to internal union dissidence in an economic context in which slack labor market conditions in many sectors provide a ready supply of replacement workers."[67]

Exceptions exist, but the tendency is for long time incumbents, who have surrounded themselves with loyalists, to speak for their unions. Ratification of collective contracts, which are typically renewed every two years, is accomplished with, at best, pro forma participation by the membership. And union elections often entail voting not by secret ballot but by a show of hands in the menacing presence of the incumbents' strongmen. The average Mexican worker quickly learns not to make waves: he pays dues, obeys orders, and hopes that his quality of life will improve.

"Exclusion clauses," first introduced in 1934 to safeguard unions against scabs, have been used as swords and shields by official leaders to attack some opponents and to thwart the aspirations of other challengers. The clauses have enabled the most important unions to protect their organizations and leaders by ousting adversaries from the unions and then having them fired and blacklisted. That these *charros* control both the dues paid by members and financial contributions provided by the government further strengthens their grip on power, thereby explaining the presence of eight septagenarians and octagenarians at the head of 73 CTM state federations and industrial unions.

Government-selected union representatives sit on the National Tripartite Commission, which sets the minimum wage for each state and the Federal District. Officers of progovernment unions also serve on the national and state arbitration boards that determine whether strikes are legal or illegal; participants in an illegal strike suffer consequences that range from losing withheld wages and unemployment benefits to facing troops dispatched as strikebreakers. In theory, the legality of a work stoppage depends on a union's adherence to certain procedures, including a properly conducted strike vote among the organization's membership. In practice, the 700-page *Ley Federal del Trabajo*, which was enacted in 1931 pursuant to Article 124 of the Constitution and amended in 1970, is sufficiently detailed to ensure the ministry and its subordinate agencies enormous discretion in interpreting the code's provisions.[68]

Before state agencies consider the merits of a strike, an elaborate minuet unfolds.[69] The steps in this labor dance include a union's formally notifying the government of its grievance, soliciting a response from management, pausing for attempts at mediation, deciding to register a prospective strike, waiting again for possible conciliation to occur, and, finally, striking. Conciliation and arbitration boards have three options in judging a strike under their jurisdiction: it may be "illegal," "nonexistent," or "legal." The first permits employers to discharge workers at will; if the union continues the work stoppage, it risks police or armed forces intervention. A nonexistent strike is one that the board determines has no legal basis because it will upset the "equilibrium among the diverse factors of production" and threaten the "balance between the rights of labor and those of capital." In such cases, employees must return to their jobs within 48 hours. Workers are unable to recoup lost wages in either illegal or nonexistent strikes. Only in strikes declared legal does the employer compensate employees for days lost from work. Weeks may elapse before boards reach decisions concerning the status of strikes. In view of the high stakes involved, unions often prefer to settle disputes peaceably or to obtain assurances of the government's sympathy before pulling their members out of a factory or mine.[70]

Opportunities for discretion and favoritism permeate the government's power to settle labor disputes by decree when orthodox conciliation procedures have not proved fruitful. Ultimately, intractable labor leaders may bear the brunt of draconian criminal sanctions. The most notorious case was in 1959 and involved Demetrio Vallejo, secretary-general of the Railroad Workers' Union. When he persisted in a strike deemed illegal, the government arrested him on vague subversion charges. Vallejo was finally brought to trial in 1964 and convicted of violating the Law of Social Dissolution, which equated political dissent with sedition. He served only 4 years of his 16-year sentence because of international pressure, and the Mexican Congress repealed the statute during the Echeverría administration.[71]

CTM Services to the State

In return for government backing, the CTM performs invaluable functions for the state. First, even in the face of declining wages, Velázquez discourages strikes and other forms of work stoppages. On numerous occasions, he has pressed the government to grant large wage increases only to settle for substantially less when it appeared that his demands would exacerbate national economic problems. For instance, Velázquez and other union officials called for nothing less than a 50 percent increase in the minimum wage in mid-1983, a year when inflation exceeded 100 percent even as the GDP fell 5 percent amid widespread unemployment. Despite the assertiveness of their demands, most leaders accepted 15 to 20 percent increases, and no major strikes erupted.[72] Despite the fact that in the 1980s Mexico suffered its worst depression since the revolution, the number of strikes declined in this period, according to the Ministry of Labor and Social Welfare. There were 675 strikes (213,531 strikers) in 1982 and 174 strikes (201,386 strikers) in 1987. Eighty-eight strikes involving 201,386 strikers occurred from January to July of 1988.[73] Table 6 presents an overview of potential and actual strikes. Between September 1986 and August 1987, unions staged only 187 of the 13,000 strikes for which notices were filed. The relatively few strikes reflected the workers' fear that management (including the state) might shut down their work place and that government-backed union leaders would not defend their rights. At the same time, joining an inde-

Table 6   Strike Activity in Mexico, 1982–1988

Year	Strikes Registered (Emplazamientos)	Strikes Carried Out (Estalladas)	Percent of Strikes Carried Out	Workers Involved in Strikes
1982	16,030	675	4.2	213,531
1983	13,536	230	1.7	125,770
1984	9,052	221	2.4	64,994
1985	8,754	125	1.4	60,841
1986	11,579	312	2.7	82,844
1987	16,142	174	1.1	201,386
1988*	3,706	88	2.4	76,854

Source: Data provided by Lic. Carlos Pérez García, Ministry of Labor and Social Welfare.

*January through July.

pendent union could mean an unsuccessful, and possibly dangerous, confrontation with the authorities.

Second, the Velázquez-led CTM has served as an effective buffer between organized labor, on one side, and Marxism and other radical ideologies, on the other. In preaching the gospel of "revolutionary nationalism," Don Fidel has extolled the role of the working class without encouraging advocates of a class struggle. After all, he is a consummate pragmatist who never tires of lauding the revolution in which he, as a teenager, fought in the ranks of Emiliano Zapata's revolutionary army. To emphasize his commitment to revolutionary nationalism, Velázquez lards his speeches with heady praise for the ruling regime and scorching criticism of its perceived enemies that include the center-right National Action Party (PAN), the Roman Catholic Church, big business, and multinational corporations.

Third, the official labor movement supports the government at critical times, such as during currency devaluations, the imposition of austerity programs, the accession to the General Agreement on Tariffs and Trade (GATT) and other controversial international organizations, presidential transitions, and such challenges to the regime's legitimacy as that presented in 1968 by students and other middle-class elements. Indeed, it is doubtful whether the PRI-dominated government could have survived the 1968 Tlatelolco confrontation had the CTM cast its lot with the university-focused protesters.[74]

The nature of the confederation's backing depends upon the circumstances. At times, Velázquez will sanction a government policy in a low-key fashion at his regular Monday news conference. On other occasions, he will make a statement at a special occasion such as those delivered every six years to unveil the PRI's presidential standard-bearer. In the early 1980s, labor preferred a candidate with a political background rather than the patently technocratic credentials of de la Madrid, the planning and budget secretary at the time of his selection. Nonetheless, in announcing de la Madrid as the party's candidate, Velázquez demonstrated that unity prevailed within the revolutionary family and that de la Madrid could count on labor's backing from the Río Grande to the Guatemalan border.

Frequently, the CTM makes common cause with a president after he has announced a controversial decision. Such was labor's enthusiastic participation in a huge rally, held in the capital's Zócalo Plaza, to endorse López Portillo's 1982 nationalization of the Mexican banking system. In the opinion of one writer, "López Portillo was looking increasingly like the bullfighter awarded both ears and the tail" because of the support for his undaunted move that was elicited from union leaders and other groups.[75] In December 1987 deteriorating economic conditions persuaded Fidel Velázquez to commit the CTM to joining the government/business/labor Economic Solidarity Pact (PSE) to combat soaring prices and to rekindle economic growth. Substantial improvements, notably in slashing the inflation rate that had climbed to 159.2 percent in 1987, persuaded Velázquez to endorse continuation of the PSE even after Salinas was inaugurated on December 1, 1988.

The fourth way the CTM helps the government is contributing candidates, manpower, money, and votes to political campaigns at the federal, state, and local levels. In July 1986 a large, solid SNTE vote helped to swell the PRI's victory total in the fiercely contested gubernatorial race in Chihuahua, and, through special school-level "brigades," SNTE leaders estimated that in 1988 they could generate more than 8 million votes for Salinas—a grossly exaggerated figure.[76] In terms of instigating marches, convocations, and demonstrations on behalf of the revolutionary party, labor is by far its most visible and effective sector. The annual May 1 "labor day" parade affords the workers' movement an institutionalized means of showing its solidarity with the government.

Thus, union leaders reveal to prominent technocratic policymakers the number of faithful who can be brought into the street and—through placards, chants, and minidemonstrations during the event—express opinions on actual or prospective programs.

Finally, labor's alliance with the PRI nourishes the mystique of Mexico's revolutionary regime. Attempts to preserve this image are especially difficult because Cárdenas's 1938 nationalization of the oil industry was the last major redistributive act in the revolutionary tradition. Moreover, land reform has long since ceased, and the purchasing power of workers plummeted during de la Madrid's term. Yet, the president and his party trumpet their links with the CTM as proof that the revolution is alive and well: "it [the visibility of leaders like Velázquez] symbolizes the presence of a unique, unbroken line of revolutionary continuity and authenticity, forged in a battle against the over-mighty leaders of big business, and it contrasts with the ever-changing upstarts of what Mexicans call the 'political class,' who have only experienced the postwar era of 'class peace.'"[77] In August 1978 the PRI formalized such symbolism by redefining itself as a "workers' party." Despite protests that the relabeling gave rise to "ideological confusion" and that the PRI was a multiclass party, the redefinition was approved. Velázquez favored the move to enhance his credibility with grass roots workers who had grown restless under the government's tough wage constraint and repression of strikes. For his part, López Portillo wanted the PRI to appear on the side of the people, especially with congressional contests scheduled for 1979. An alliance with labor—no matter how formal—was viewed as "an essential insurance policy" for the upcoming elections.[78]

The Asymmetrical Relationship

Asymmetry defines the symbiotic relationship between the regime and organized labor inasmuch as the former clearly dominates the latter. Evidence of this dominance abounds. To begin with, labor has continuously been forced to accept wage increases that fall far short of the inflation rate. Similarly, reduction in the workweek from 48 to 40 hours for all workers has yet to be realized despite the CTM's having championed this decrease for more than three decades.[79] Years of importuning aside, the confederation achieved wage indexing only in 1988, and then in a significantly modified form. In early 1982 union leaders in Congress introduced a five-point package to improve labor's plight. In addition to (1) a shorter workweek and (2) wage indexing, the projected reforms included (3) unemployment benefits, (4) employer-provided low-cost housing, and (5) an end to government meddling in strikes at state-run industries. The measures died when a PRI leader walked out of the chamber, taking with him so many deputies that the party's union wing was left without a quorum to begin debate.[80] To mollify labor, Salinas may benevolently agree to a revision of the Federal Labor Law considered "obsolete" by CTM officials.[81] Changes might include shortening the workweek, improving retirement benefits, doubling to 10 percent employer contributions to INFONAVIT, cushioning the impact of new technologies and structural reforms on union members, and expanding the social sector.

Further evidence of labor's subordinate position lies in the modest number of political posts held by union activists. Although the number of congressional seats alloted to labor by the PRI has risen modestly in recent years, it is still far below the total enjoyed by the popular sector. Moreover, the expansion of the Congress to 500 seats in 1988 means that labor's contingent as a percentage of the overall membership has declined. Too, on a proportional basis, labor suffered more legislative losses (19) than any other sector in the July 1988 national elections, including the defeat of five candidates for the Chamber of Deputies and one Senate aspirant in Mexico City. The unsuccessful Senate nominee was Joaquín Gamboa Pascoe, a Velázquez confidant and secretary-general of the Federation of Federal District Workers (FTDF). Despite these setbacks, labor representatives hold the balance of power in the 500-seat Congress where the PRI's 263 seats are but a margin over opposition parties' 237. As the seven-member contingent of Oil Workers' Union deputies demonstrated in their diatribe against Beteta, the parliament provides a valuable forum for advancing union interests. As previously mentioned, CTM leaders hold only 2 of 31 governorships, and a CTM member has never served as head (delegado) of one of the 16 delegations that compose the Federal District's administrative structure. Further, surprisingly few party leaders or agency heads have emerged from labor's ranks, with de la Madrid appointing only one trade unionist to a subcabinet post.

Despite the fact that Velázquez is consulted on possible candidates, organized labor appears to have had limited influence in the selection process since the 1940s. Even though Don Fidel publicly announced that the revolutionary family had selected de la Madrid as its presidential nominee in 1982, "the veteran kingmaker . . . suffered the indignity of finding out the candidate's identity only at the last minute."[82] Obviously, his lobbying in 1987 in behalf of del Mazo proved fruitless. Don Fidel no longer holds sway over policies that affect working people. Under López Portillo, he single-handedly blocked an increase in gasoline prices deemed onerous to his membership; however, when de la Madrid decided to raise dairy prices, Velázquez—the former milkman—was simply informed of the decision instead of being asked in advance for his advice. To raise the stock of the aging *charro* whose support is crucial in preserving social peace, some observers assumed that Salinas would place more labor stalwarts in visible administrative positions. It was believed that, while loath to award the CTM the secretary of labor portfolio that it would like, the new chief executive might allow Don Fidel to place one or more of his loyalists in subsecretarial posts in second-order ministries such as fisheries or agriculture and hydraulic resources.

No such appointments were made. In fact, Salinas named a cabinet that can be expected to stand fast in the face of labor's escalating demands. He reappointed as labor secretary the tough-minded Farell Cubillas whom union leaders may respect for his firmness but for whom they feel no affection. Pedro Aspe Armella, a staunch proponent of economic liberalization, will serve as finance secretary. And former interior secretary, Manuel Barlett Díaz, a strong-willed, tenacious negotiator was assigned the education portfolio, which invests him with the responsibility for relations with the large and vociferous unions of teachers (SNTE) and university workers (STUNAM). The new interior secretary, Fernando Gutiérrez Barrios, is a hard-as-nails political veteran who will unflinchingly carry out the internal security functions assigned to his ministry.

6

Looking toward the Future

Fidel Velázquez is, despite his declining influence, the undisputed leader of his nation's labor movement and one of the half-dozen most powerful men in Mexico. Born in Villa Nicolas Romero in Mexico state, he participated in the revolution before beginning work as a *lechero* (dairyman) on the Hacienda del Rosario. In 1921 he was fired "for having begun to encourage the creation of a union to defend us against the exploitation to which we were subjected."[83] Three years later, he helped organize the Syndical Union of Dairy Industry Workers (USTIL). This organization immediately joined CROM, which had become the nation's strongest central labor body thanks to support received from Obregón and Calles. Velázquez broke with the extravagantly ambitious Morones and allied himself with the leftist Lombardo Toledano to form the CTM.

Velázquez, assisted by the other four *lobitos*, secured the position of secretary of organization and propaganda. He used this key post both to consolidate his power and to vault himself into the secretary-generalship, replacing Toledano in 1941. Despite Fernando Ampila, another *lobito*, assuming the secretary-generalship in 1947, Velázquez remained the power behind the throne, returning to the formal leadership of the CTM in 1948, and retaining it to this day.

In the opinion of his admirers, Don Fidel has promoted labor unity, contributed to a favorable environment for economic growth, encouraged cohesion within the PRI, and symbolized the revolution. According to López Portillo, "The history of Mexico cannot be understood without Fidel Velázquez. He is an extraordinary and exceptional leader as well as an exemplary patriot and magnificent Mexican."[84] In contrast, critics attack the tall, sunglasses-wearing Velázquez for continually yielding to the government on wage demands, for insensitivity to the plight of peasants and nonunionized workers, for ignoring corruption that is rife within the labor movement, and for resisting democratization of either the CTM or the PRI.

64

Still, advocates and detractors agree that the 89-year-old curmudgeon has contributed mightily to the social peace that Mexico has enjoyed for the last half-century. Will his retirement or death unleash centrifugal forces that could shatter the labor movement and, in turn, threaten the nation's stability? The transition to the next CTM leader will not be easy. For both obvious and subtle reasons, no one can fill Don Fidel's shoes. After all, he fought in the revolution, enjoyed enormous freedom of action because of his support from Lázaro Cárdenas and Avila Camacho, and played a key role in creating the CTM, which he has shaped to fit his leadership style. During the last four decades, Velázquez has personally appointed or approved everyone of importance in the CTM's ever larger bureaucracy. Additionally, in the 1930s and early 1940s, the national presidency was not nearly as much of an institutionalized restraint as it is now on the activities of a shrewdly ambitious labor leader. Moreover, Velázquez's rapid ascent in the labor movement was impelled by his support from the compact group of *lobitos*—for which there is no present-day counterpart to loft the star of a would-be secretary-general.

In fact, the next group of CTM leaders is far less impressive than those of Velázquez's generation, in large measure because they have not been permitted to undertake bold initiatives in view of Don Fidel's awesome presence. At times, the confederation's inner sanctum appears as Byzantine and impenetrable as the Kremlin. Yet, a medley of factors suggests that the CTM—though materially weakened—could survive intact when Velázquez passes from the scene. First, although certain leaders of industrial unions—the now-discredited SRTPRM's Hernández Galicia and the SUTERM's Leonardo Rodríguez Alcaine—would relish succeeding Velázquez, the CTM's 40 industrial unions suffer personal rivalries, programmatic differences, and an overall lack of cooperation that militate against their agreeing on a rival to the incumbent's handpicked successor. Second, the pragmatism that Don Fidel has infused in the CTM should work against an ideological conflict sundering the organization once he leaves the picture. The Arturo Romo faction may field a candidate at the CTM's next convention in 1992; however, in the absence of social turmoil, it is doubtful that this contingent will seek to challenge the governance of an interim secretary-general should Velázquez leave office before his term expires. Third, a veritable gerontocracy of state CTM chiefs—some of whom have groomed their own successors—should provide continuity when Velázquez steps aside. Conspicuous in this group are Heliodoro Hernández Loza (Jalisco), Raúl Caballero Escamilla (Nuevo León), Antonio Ramírez Martínez (Durango), and Salvador Durán Pérez (Chiapas). Fourth, Salinas will take action to prevent the CTM's being plunged into a protracted and bloody succession struggle. He can be expected to use force if incentives do not ensure a satisfactory transition that produces a moderate, progovernment secretary-general. On balance, the PRI-dominated regime can do more for the *charros* than vice versa. This dependence, noted earlier, is especially prominent now that the labor "dinosaurs," as they are derisively called, have so little rapport with their much younger rank and file, many of whom believe that they have been sold out by corrupt, aged leaders. Contempt for their leaders drove large numbers of union members, especially FSTSE and blue-collar workers in Mexico City and other urban areas, to back Cárdenas for president just as millions of North American hard-hats ignored AFL-CIO endorsements of Jimmy Carter and Walter Mondale and supported Ronald Reagan in 1980 and 1984. Finally, Velázquez appears to have chosen his successor—a factor that is enormously important within the labor elite in legitimizing a new CTM head.

Velázquez keeps his cards close to his ample paunch lest the announcement of a political heir convert him into a lame duck and accelerate intramural maneuvering. Nonetheless, signals abound that Senator Emilio M. González Parra, governor of Nayarit until 1987, is his preferred interim replacement. Evidence of this choice lies in González's having (1) presided over the 1986 CTM convention that elected Velázquez to this current six-year term, (2) sat next to him at the 25,000-delegate conclave, (3) been selected the second alternate secretary-general (the number one alternate is the 81-year-old Blas Chumacero Sánchez, who is not a contender for secretary-general), (4) directed the CTM's participation in Salinas's presidential campaign, and (5) been named to head PRI's 60-member delegation in the 64-seat Senate to which the former governor was elected in mid-1988.[85] Further enhancing his prospects are the losses experienced by other CTM leaders—losses by Pascoe Gamboa and Romo or the tainted victories of de la Vega, Osorio, Rodríguez Alcaine, and petrochemical workers head Muñoz Mósqueda—in the elections from which González emerged with an overwhelming, undisputed victory.

Born in 1913, González is a Velázquez loyalist who speaks well, approaches issues pragmatically, and enjoys respect among colleagues for having emerged from the ranks of workers rather than having entered the labor movement as a technocrat. Still, as longtime head of the Nayarit Workers' Federation (FTN), he will meet resistance from heads of industrial unions who would like one of their own, rather than a product of a geographic federation, to succeed Velázquez. Still, industrial union chiefs will be hesitant to mount a challenge that could shake the very foundation of organized labor at a time when harsh economic conditions nourish unrest among their rank and file, and—at least at present—no organization outside the CTM can successfully compete for leadership of the labor movement.

Some strategically placed unions can mitigate the impact on their members of the structural changes now occurring in Mexico. In general, however, the rising unemployment likely to continue during the wider promulgation of an export-focused growth model will place labor organizations at a disadvantage in bargaining sessions. Moreover, the Mexican economy is changing in such a manner that the number of unionized employees is declining as a percentage of the labor force while the absolute number of workers is expanding—a fact that means even greater competition for scarce jobs. This growth is concentrated in the 1,400 *maquiladora* twin-assembly plants and other service industries whose employees, like their U.S. counterparts, are notoriously difficult to organize. Except in Matamoros, where Agapito González Cavazos, a shrewd *charro*, has promised the operating firms labor peace in exchange for acquiescing in his organizing efforts, the young females who constitute the bulk of *maquiladora* workers remain beyond the union pale. Furthermore, the stronger emphasis on market forces inherent in structural reform and the efforts to combat corruption are working to the detriment of sweetheart arrangements that many syndicates—the Oil Workers' Union (STRPRM), for example—have forged with their employers. The STRPRM's savage attack on former Pemex director-general Beteta for having committed "treason against the president and robbery of the nation" was La Quina's transparent effort to put Salinas on the defensive in hopes of dissuading the young president from cleaning up the Augean stable that the petroleum sector has become.

Labor is also aghast at Salinas's proposal that political "modernization" complement the economic restructuring. Above all, the newly elected chief executive wants to alter Mexico's image as a country that practices democracy 364 days a year—with election day as the only exception! In his campaign speeches, he acknowledged obliquely that in some northern states, the official party had been declared victorious at the expense of its credibility. Thus, he called for clean elections to ensure peaceful change in this nation of 85 million people. Implicit in that pledge was a repudiation of vote padding, which the PRI had frequently practiced when faced with anemic victory margins or likely defeats. "The rejection of obsolete practices and electoral vices comes not only from the PRI's candidate for the presidency but from the majority of Mexicans," he said. "We are therefore going to respect the citizens' vote and carry out clean and transparent elections."[86] "Reform implies risks, but risks are better than not doing anything. I prefer the risk of reform to the risk of inactivity." In addition, he averred that "I'm not looking to break a record for the number of votes, but a record for credibility in the electoral results. For me that's the most important thing."[87] As strong opposition became evident, Salinas told the party faithful that the era of one-party rule "is ending" and that a new period of "intense political competition" has begun.[88]

What changes might be undertaken to enhance the PRI's attractiveness to the millions of Mexicans who believe that it is simply a coercive instrument to provide power, wealth, and perquisites to a self-serving leadership? Reformers have advanced a number of ideas, some of which have been accepted by the party's leadership. Their proposals include recruiting better candidates; using primary elections and other techniques to open up a candidate selection process traditionally accomplished by the *dedazo* (handpicking) of nominees by party elites; revamping the party's corporatist pyramid; welcoming women, young people, and political newcomers to party affairs; negotiating with opponents; and—of course—respecting the genuine outcome of elections. Manuel Camacho Solís, a member of Salinas's inner circle and PRI's secretary-general until he was appointed mayor of Mexico City on December 1, 1988, insists that the party must stop serving as a rubber stamp for the government and become the "major interlocutor with society and a permanent and active bridge between society and government."[89]

Nevertheless, hundreds of veteran bosses are aghast over the gravitation of power since the 1970s from the PRI to the bureaucracy. They resent having reforms thrust upon them by foreign-educated technocrats. Such men and women have never dirtied their hands in the political trenches; nonetheless, they arrogantly disdain old-line politicos as undemocratic hacks who only know how to enrich themselves and fix elections. For many *charros* and other PRI diehards, an intrusive state generates invaluable political resources, and elections offer a convenient device both to transfer the presidential sash peacefully from one *jefe máximo* (big chief) to another and to legitimize the party's grip on power. Such contests were never intended to allow opposition victories. Rather, the *carro completo* (clean sweep) enables labor chieftains and their peasant counterparts to reward their loyalists.

For this reason, labor and other elements of the PRI's old guard unsuccessfully attempted to convince Camacho Solís that Salinas should be awarded a hefty electoral triumph, not a bare majority, both as proof of the official party's continued ascendancy and as evidence that Cárdenas's political prospects were nil. The younger technocrats perceived that gross vote inflation would erode even more the legitimacy of the PRI, which is scorned by the urban poor, grass roots workers, university students, important elements of the business community and middle class, many northerners, and other groups who feel unrepresented by an organization viewed as a venal political museum piece.

Thus, key actors have decried the notion of continuing de la Madrid-sponsored economic *perestroika* (restructuring) much less embarking on *glasnost*-like (openness) political changes. Traditional CTM leaders fear that free elections will threaten their members' pocketbooks, their own privileged positions, and the preservation of notoriously undemocratic intraunion procedures. For example, on the question of attenuating PRI's corporatist organization, Fidel Velázquez proclaimed, "We will never accept the party's acting at the margin of the sectors," as proposed by "a pseudo-ideologue"—a mordant rebuke of Camacho Solís.[90] Velázquez became livid when Mexico City PRI chairman Jesús Salazar Toledano, a stalwart of the party's middle-class "popular" sector, attempted to cross sectoral lines to involve union members in mobilizing activities in the capital where the official party suffered a stinging defeat in the July 1988 elections.

In addition, inefficient manufacturers fear that restructuring could spark competition from more efficient producers; FSTSE-affiliated bureaucrats fear that reducing the state's economic role will diminish the influence and opportunities derived from dispensing import permits, setting quotas, and performing thousands of regulatory functions; many intellectuals fear that encouraging market forces will enhance the influence of despised domestic and foreign capitalists; and, many PRI barons fear that expanding the private sector at the expense of the state will shrink the patronage and boodle needed to lubricate the party's creaky machinery. No greater challenge confronts Salinas than that of broadening a now modest coalition—one that embraces large, efficient producers, the international financial community, some intellectuals, and many high-level technocrats in ministries with economic functions—to advance the reforms for which de la Madrid laid the groundwork.

Velázquez's successor will find it increasingly difficult to perform the dual roles of pillar of the regime and advocate for one-quarter of the work force. The representatives of workers will be preoccupied, as they are now, trying to preserve jobs and purchasing power in the face of increasingly high unemployment. This will leave labor with virtually no time or energy to concentrate on a broader political agenda in Mexico's extremely hierarchical system. Even more than their independent counterparts, however, official labor leaders have shown virtually no ability to expand their demands beyond narrow bread-and-butter issues at a time of extremely serious economic conditions. In 1988 the minimum wage lagged behind inflation for the sixth straight year, as workers' paychecks shrunk; open and disguised unemployment beset nearly half of the nation's workers; the foreign debt approached $105 billion; many subsidies were being phased out even as the price of such essentials as gasoline, electricity, transportation, and food was rising. In October 1987 the Mexican stock index plunged as much as 75 percent, a month later the peso fell 25 percent against the dollar as the Central Bank—anxious to conserve its hard currency reserves—withdrew its support for the peso on the secondary or "free" market; and ubiquitous pollution continued to contaminate the already fetid air of Mexico City and other urban centers.

Similar conditions in the United States or Western Europe would have ignited demonstrations, detonated strikes, and launched the careers of demagogic politicians. Nevertheless, Mexico remained remarkably quiet. Discontent was manifested largely by opposition politicians and union leaders denouncing the Economic Solidarity Pact and by journalistic condemnations: bristling editorials in *Unomásuno*, *La Jornada*, and other leftist newspapers and muckraking articles in *Proceso* about antinationalistic and corrupt acts by government officials. Roman Catholic Church and the National Action Party leaders criticized the regime, petty crime increased in Mexico City, and acute cynicism and pessimism registered both in public opinion surveys and in voter abstention. Many Salinas confidants as well as the self-described *Critical Current*, successor to Cuauhtémoc Cárdenas's *Democratic Current*, demanded reform of the PRI.

Growing worker unrest and the likely upsurge in activities by independent unions, especially in the north, could sharpen pressures for democratization of the CTM, parallel to that taking place in the PRI. For the *charros*, the prospect of internal reform is the political equivalent of fingernails clawing a blackboard. Still, the inertness of the average union member, long the object of paternalism, reduces the impact of such democratizing forces.

Even amid mounting tensions, several factors work against general strikes or other forms of worker activism that would imperil the stability of the system. First, the barter or *economía subterránea* (underground) economy expanded to the point that it equaled 25 to 35 percent of GDP in the mid-1980s. Although the underground transactions deprived the national treasury of resources equivalent to 26 percent of the revenues, the transactions help buffer the hardship endured by millions of Mexicans.[91] Second, extended families—often with several members working full-time and others selling artificial flowers, washing windshields, or hawking lottery tickets—provide a safety net for the jobless. Third, for Mexicans, the most attractive welfare scheme is a porous U.S. frontier across which nearly 1.2 million illegal immigrants passed in 1987. In December 1986, President Reagan signed an immigration reform bill, but so flexible are its provisions—notably with respect to agricultural workers—that the legislation has only slowed the heavy influx of unlawful workers.[92]

Even though it may be galvanizing for Cárdenas to have been awarded 31.1 percent of the vote in the bitterly disputed 1988 presidential contest, political cannibalism has engulfed the left. Over the years, hard-liners have competed with Eurocommunists for leadership of the PSUM, a left-wing amalgam that captured only 3.2 percent of the 1985 congressional elections. The PSUM and four other leftist parties, which joined together to form the Mexican Socialist Party (PMS) in 1987, found it difficult to work in harness behind a single candidate in the 1988 campaign.[93] Therefore, the PMS nominee, Heberto Castillo, dropped out of the race in early June and threw his support to Cárdenas. The PMS failed to capture a seat in the Chamber of Deputies, further indicating the public's anti-Marxism. Cárdenas may have better luck in uniting the left behind his Party of the Democratic Revolution (PRD), organized in October 1988. But spokesmen for several of the groupings that endorsed Cárdenas's presidential bid expressed reluctance to submerge their organizations in the new party.

Thus far, the knowledge that violence accomplishes nothing politically and that the army will brook no guerrilla adventurism has kept extremists in the PMS, the PRT, and the Castro-oriented *Corriente Socialista* from trading ballots for bullets. An exception has been the miniscule Vicente Guerrero Revolutionary Command, which in May 1987 claimed credit for an explosion in front of the PRI's Mexico City headquarters. An ambulance owned by the party was destroyed and the building's windows were shattered by the blast.[94] The death of more than one million people in the 1910 revolution—a fact that adults learned from grandparents who vividly remember the carnage—has sensitized Mexicans to the danger inherent in widespread violence. The Tlatelolco massacre in 1968 provides a more recent reminder of the regime's willingness to use force in a confrontation.

Finally, the 145,000-member armed forces—though top-heavy with senior officers and hardly of Prussian caliber—have started to transform themselves into a modern military. Jeeps and trucks have replaced horses in all but two ceremonial cavalry units; five armored regiments boast personnel carriers and light Panhand tanks; German-designed G-3 automatic rifles have been introduced in the army's 86 infantry battalions; and the air force, which is a branch of the army, has acquired a dozen F-5 supersonic aircraft. Military leaders continue to trumpet their loyalty to a political system that has co-opted them with a lavish array of social and economic perquisites. Even more worrisome than an organized challenge to the system is the remote possibility that a spontaneous demonstration in one part of Mexico City over, say, higher tortilla prices or bus fares could spread like wildfire across the capital and then to other cities, unimpeded by the firebreak of legitimacy essential to any regime's survival. Still, a loyal military along with government control over the mass media should curb anomic disturbances. Arguably, "too many Mexicans have a stake in social tranquility and political continuity for a politician or faction to find fertile ground for rebellion, *pronunciamientos*, or radical breaks with the status quo."[95]

While Salinas should not have to worry about revolution, his successor may have to rely heavily on the military to handle social violence unless prompt action is taken to restore the regime's standing with the people. Political reform—as significant as it may be to the new chief executive's technocratic advisers—is of secondary importance to relieving the acute economic distress endured by the great majority of Mexico's long-suffering population. The Economic Solidarity Pact has sharply reduced inflation. Yet, renewed growth is essential to creating employment and imbuing the beleaguered regime with legitimacy. Absent a sharp rise in oil prices or some other fortuitous event, such growth is impossible as long as Mexico expends $12 billion annually in interest and amortization on its external debt.

By acting decisively against Hernández Galicia, who is the dark side of Mexican politics, Salinas has made clear that a resuscitated presidency will exercise all of the power at its disposal to implement the structural reforms so crucial to his nation's advancement. The business community and international bankers learned that the president, backed to the hilt by the military, is determined to manage events rather than be overtaken by them. He has also sent a message to organized labor that they should not resist the continued belt-tightening inherent in his liberalization program. Above all, the youthful chief executive has shed the image of an eggheaded technocrat for that of a *hombre fuerte* (strongman) whom the public and power brokers alike must respect even if they do not like him and his market-oriented policies. In terms of perceptions, throwing La Quina and his cronies in jail was Salinas's PATCO strike and Grenada invasion fused into one gutsy move. Yet, the political and psychological benefits of his action endure for only a couple of months unless complemented by serious relief for a country whose economic well-being is vital to U.S. security.

Hence, Salinas's highest priority must be to strike a deal with the international financial community whereby a significant percentage of the debt is written off, swapped for equity holdings, converted into "exit bonds," or transformed into long-term securities guaranteed by the World Bank or a similar institution. A breakthrough on the debt question would raise Salinas's popularity, undercut Cárdenas's most salient issue, give a psychological fillip to a timid private sector whose support is crucial to economic restructuring, and stimulate development. Both the creditor banks' intractability and the change of administrations in Washington militate against speedy action. Growth and emphasis on supply-and-demand forces may impel political liberalization as individuals who enjoy more decision-making opportunities in the economic realm can be expected to demand more choices in political matters. In other words, *perestroika* could open the door to *glasnost*. Salinas's readiness to moderate political reforms and to make overtures to labor should enable the regime to receive, at times begrudgingly, the continued support of the *charros*, provided that they do not—like La Quina—break the rule of Mexico's Byzantine political game. The majority of *charros* realizes that cooperation with the government is crucial to preserving their influence in a society where the union movement's influence is declining.

Of course, should Salinas assign equal importance to restructuring and democratization, he may—without brisk economic growth—provoke such turmoil that Cárdenas's PRD would become the odds-on favorite to capture the 1991 congressional elections. This prospect would prompt some CTM union heads to defect to Cárdenas lest they be thrown out of office by an increasingly embittered rank and file whose tolerance for hardship is limited. Meanwhile, CTM *charros* and other members of the PRI's old guard would resist to their last breath the handing over of Congress to Cárdenas whom Velázquez considers a traitor to both his father Lázaro's memory and the revolutionary tradition. Doubtless, they would favor calling on the military, if necessary, to impose a PRI victory in the 1991 legislative contests and in the 1993 presidential election. Arturo Romo has even floated the idea of forming a "workers' party" to safeguard the interests of union members and peasants that he believes the free-enterprise, cosmopolitan technocrats running PRI ignore. Although unlikely, this possibility was unthinkable six years ago and appears improbable as long as Fidel Velázquez is around to promote cohesion. That the idea of a workers' party is being circulated underscores the gravity and high stakes of the political situation facing Salinas, who entered office as Mexico's weakest chief executive in nearly 60 years. Pursuing sweeping political changes before achieving healthy, sustained growth could further divide the revolutionary family and convert longtime PRI loyalists into detractors of a government that they helped to elect but believe has betrayed them. Under such circumstances, *perestroika* might encourage *glasnost* only to engender *volnenye* (conflict), not stability and peace.[96]

Notes

1. Interview with Miguel de la Madrid Hurtado, Mexico City, November 11, 1987.
2. For a discussion of the document, *Lineamientos para un programa básico de la revolución mexicana en el período 1988-1994*, see *Proceso*, September 7, 1987, pp. 6-11.
3. *New York Times*, February 6, 1984, p. A-7.
4. *Proceso*, November 9, 1987, p. 9.
5. *Proceso*, July 25, 1988, pp. 26-29.
6. For works on the history of organized labor in Mexico, see Víctor Alba, *Politics and the Labor Movement in Latin America* (Stanford, Calif.: Stanford University Press, 1968); Robert J. Alexander, *Organized Labor in Latin America* (Toronto: The Free Press, 1965); Rodney D. Anderson, *Outcasts in Their Own Land: Mexican Industrial Workers 1906-1911* (Dekalb, Ill.: Northern Illinois University Press, 1976); Joe C. Ashby, *Organized Labor and the Mexican Revolution under Lázaro Cárdenas* (Chapel Hill, N.C.: University of North Carolina Press, 1967); Jorge Basurto, *La clase obrera en la historia de méxico, en el régimen de echeverría: rebelión e independencia* (Mexico City: Siglo Veintiuno Editores, 1983); Luis Adolfo Santaibáñez Belmont, *CTM: a la vanguardia de la revolución* (Puebla de Zaragoza, 1984); Dan La Botz, *The Crisis of Mexican Labor* (New York: Praeger, 1988); Manuel Camacho, *La clase obrera en la historia de méxico: el futuro inmediato* (Mexico City: Siglo Veintiuno Editores, 1980); George W. Grayson, *The Politics of Mexican Oil* (Pittsburgh: University of Pittsburgh Press, 1980); Instituto de Investigaciones, *El obrero mexicano* (a series): (1) *demografía y condiciones de vida*, (2) *condiciones de trabajo*, (3) *organización sindicalismo*, (4) *el derecho laboral*, and (5) *la política y la cultura* (Mexico City: Siglo Veintiuno Editores, 1985); Kevin J. Middlebrook, *The Political Economy of Mexican Organized Labor* (Ann Arbor, Mich.: University Microfilms International, 1982); Partido Revolucionario Institucional, *50 años de lucha obrera* (Mexico City: Instituto de Capacitación Política, 1986); Ian Roxborough, *Unions and Politics in Mexico* (Cambridge: Cambridge University Press, 1984); Ramón Eduardo Ruiz, *Labor and the Ambivalent Revolutionaries: Mexico, 1911-1923* (Baltimore: Johns Hopkins Univer-

sity Press, 1976); Hobart A. Spalding, *Organized Labor in Latin America* (New York: Harper and Row, 1977); and Virginia López Villegas-Manjarrez, *La ctm vs. las organizaciones obreras* (Mexico City: Ediciones El Caballito, 1983).

7. Alba, *Politics and the Labor Movement in Latin America*, 53.

8. Howard F. Cline, *The United States and Mexico* (New York: Atheneum, 1965), 117.

9. Alexander, *Organized Labor in Latin America*, 184.

10. With respect to the La Cananea and Río Blanco-Orizaba strikes, see Rodney D. Anderson, *Outcasts in Their Own Land*, pp. 110-117 and 282-297.

11. La Botz, *The Crisis of Mexican Labor* (New York: Praeger, 1988), 16-17.

12. Cited in Marjorie Ruth Clark, *Organized Labor in Mexico* (New York: Russell & Russell, 1973), 37.

13. Middlebrook, *The Political Economy of Mexican Organized Labor, 1940-1978*, 51.

14. Spalding, Jr., *Organized Labor in Latin America*, 101.

15. Roxborough, *Unions and Politics in Mexico,* 12.

16. La Botz, *The Crisis of Mexican Labor*, 25.

17. Amos J. Peaslee, "Constitution of Mexico," in *Constitutions of Nations* (The Netherlands: Martinus Nijhoff, 1956), 702-705.

18. Roxborough, *Unions and Politics in Mexico*, 13.

19. Jorge Basurto, *El proletariado industrial en méxico, 1850-1930* (Mexico City: National Autonomous University of Mexico, 1975), 172-173, 202-205, 209-210, 243 and cited in Middlebrook, *The Political Economy of Mexican Organized Labor*, 53.

20. Basurto, *El proletariado industrial*, 209-214 and cited in Middlebrook, *The Political Economy of Mexican Organized Labor*, 55-56.

21. Spalding, *Organized Labor in Latin America*, 105.

22. La Botz, *The Crisis of Mexican Labor*, 52-53.

23. Roxborough, *Unions and Politics in Mexico*, 17.

24. Middlebrook, *The Political Economy of Mexican Organized Labor*, 62.

25. Ashby, *Organized Labor and the Mexican Revolution under Lázaro Cárdenas*, 26.

26. Middlebrook, *The Political Economy of Mexican Organized Labor*, 66.

27. Michael C. Meyer and William L. Sherman, *The Course of Mexican History* (New York: Oxford University Press, 1983), 629.

28. Roxborough, *Unions and Politics in Mexico*, 23.

29. Confederación de Trabajadores de México, *Constitución* (Mexico City: CTM, 1986), 25ff.

30. Camacho, *La clase obrera en la historia de méxico: el futuro inmediato*, 118.

31. Javier Freyre Rubio, *Las organizaciones sindicales, obreras y burocráticas contemporáneas en méxico* (Mexico City: National Autonomous Metropolitana-Azcapotzalco, 1983).

32. Confederación Revolucionaria de Obreras y Campesinos, *Estatutos* (Mexico City: CROC, 1980), 29 ff.

33. For a description of the November 10, 1988 shoot-out, see *Proceso*, November 14, 1988, pp. 20-23.

34. Rubio, *Las organizaciones sindicales*.

35. James D. Rudolph, ed., *Mexico: A Country Study* (Washington, D.C.: GPO, 1985), 270.

36. *Proceso*, November 14, 1988, p. 23.

37. Roxborough, *Unions and Politics in Mexico*, 78-79.

38. Frank Brandenburg, *The Making of Modern Mexico* (Englewood Cliffs, N.J.: Prentice-Hall, 1964), 121.

39. Interview with Mario Suárez, Secretary General of the Revolutionary Confederation of Workers, Mexico City, August 23, 1988.

40. Juan Felipe Leal, "Las estructuras sindicales," in *El obrero mexicano* (Mexico City: Siglo Veintiuno, 1985), 57.

41. Barry Carr, "The Mexican Economic Debacle and the Labor Movement: A New Era or More of the Same?", Donald L. Wyman (ed.), *Mexico's Economic Crisis*, monograph prepared for the Center for U.S.-Mexican Studies, University of California at San Diego, 1983, p. 93.

42. STERM, *Insurgencia obrera y nacionalismo revolucionario* (Mexico City: Ediciones El Caballito, 1973), 31; quoted in La Botz, *The Crisis of Mexican Labor*, 136.

43. Carr, "The Mexican Economic Debacle," 93.

44. Ibid., 94.

45. Leal, "Las estructuras sindicales," 59.

46. U.S. Department of Labor, "Foreign Labor Trends, 1986-87," American Embassy, Mexico City, 16.

47. Roxborough, *Unions and Politics in Mexico*, 33; "Unions in Mexico: Who They Are," *Business Mexico* (August 1985), 76.

48. La Botz, *The Crisis of Mexican Labor*, 127.

49. "Unions in Mexico: Who They Are," 76.

50. U.S. Department of Labor, "Foreign Labor Trends," 18.

51. Alexander, *Organized Labor in Latin America*, 192.

52. Of the 33 CT affiliates, 2 belong to the PRI, 25 have leaders who are members of the official party, and 6 are independent.

53. César Zazueta and Ricardo de la Peña, *La estructura del congreso del trabajo* (Mexico City: Fondo de Cultura Económica, 1984), 104-105.

54. Middlebrook introduces the concept of political, economic, and legal subsidies in *The Political Economy of Mexican Organized Labor*, 99 ff.

55. Ibid., 101.

56. Interview with Hebraicaz Vázquez Gutiérrez, Mexico City, May 31, 1978.

57. *New York Times*, July 31, 1978, p. A-3.

58. Carr, "The Mexican Economic Debacle," 100.

59. *Proceso*, November 14, 1988, pp. 20-23.

60. From the CTM newspaper *Ceteme* and cited in Middlebrook, *The Political Economy of Mexican Organized Labor*, 113.

61. Ibid., 114.

62. La Botz, *The Crisis of Mexican Labor*, 82.

63. Rudolph, *Mexico: A Country Study*, 151.

64. *Ceteme*, August 30, 1988, p. 11.

65. Carr, "The Mexican Economic Debacle," 98.

66. Grayson, *The Politics of Mexican Oil*, 91-92.

67. Middlebrook, *The Political Economy of Mexican Organized Labor*, 118.

68. Secretaria del Trabajo y Previsión Social, *Ley federal del trabajo* (Mexico City: STPS, 1986), 297 ff.

69. Spalding, *Organized Labor in Mexico*, 135.

70. Ibid.

71. Martin C. Needler, *Mexican Politics: the Containment of Conflict* (New York: Praeger, 1982), 62-63; and Spalding, *Organized Labor in Latin America*, 137.

72. *New York Times*, January 29, 1984, p. E-5.

73. Data obtained from Lic. Carlos Pérez García, Ministry of Labor and Social Welfare, Mexico City, August 25, 1988.

74. Manuel Camacho, *La clase obrera en la historia de méxico: el futuro inmediato*, 114.

75. *Latin American Weekly Report*, November 19, 1982, p. 6.

76. Raul Trejo Delarbre, "La paralisis obrera," *Nexos* (April 1987): 61.

77. Carr, "The Mexican Economic Debacle," 99.

78. The definition of "worker" was so inclusive that anyone who held any job would be included. Workers were said to be "in general all Mexicans who contribute to the creation or distribution of material and cultural goods and social services by means of the application of their labor power"; see, *Latin America Political Report*, August 18, 1978, p. 255.

79. Collective contracts in major industries do stipulate a 40-hour workweek for union members covered by the accords.

80. *Facts on File*, February 12, 1982, p. 99.

81. Interview with Alfonso G. Calderón Velarde, Third Alternate Secretary-General, CTM, Mexico City, August 23, 1988.

82. *Latin America Weekly Report*, October 9, 1981, p. 10.

83. Carlos Velasco, *Fidel velázquez* (n.p.: Plaza & James, 1986), 8.

84. Riding, *Distant Neighbors*, 85.

85. *Proceso*, March 3, 1986, pp. 12-19.

86. *Financial Times*, May 26, 1988, p. 4.

87. *Washington Post*, May 12, 1988, p. A-23.

88. *New York Times*, July 10, 1988, p. A-15.

89. *Proceso*, August 8, 1988, p. 15.

90. *Proceso*, September 5, 1988, p. 33.

91. Centro de Estudios Económicos del Sector Privado A.C., "La economía subterránea en méxico," *Actividad Económica*, 103 (September 1986).

92. *Washington Post*, July 9, 1987, p. A-16.

93. *Latin American Weekly Report*, April 9, 1987, p. 8.

94. *Daily Report (Latin America)*, May 6, 1987, p. M-5.

95. Jorge G. Castañeda, "Mexico's Coming Challenges," *Foreign Policy* 64 (Fall 1986): 134.

96. For this insight, I am indebted to John J. Bailey, Associate Professor of Government, Georgetown University.

Glossary of Names of Worker Organizations Political Parties

BUO   Worker Unity Bloc (*Bloque de Unidad Obrera*)

CGOCM   General Confederation of Mexican Workers and Peasants (*Confederación General de Obreros y Campesinos de México*)

CGT   General Confederation of Workers (*Confederación General de Trabajadores*)

CNCT   Catholic National Confederation of Labor (*Confederación Nacional Católica del Trabajo*)

CNT   National Chamber of Labor (*Cámara Nacional de Trabajo*)

CNTE   Coordinating Committee of Educational Workers (*Coordinadora Nacional de Trabajadores de la Educación*)

COM   House of the World's Workers (*Casa del Obrero Mundial*)

COR   The Revolutionary Workers' Confederation (*Confederación Obrera Revolucionaria*)

CROC   Revolutionary Confederation of Workers and Peasants (*Confederación Revolucionaria de Obreros y Campesinos*)

CROM   Regional Confederation of Mexican Workers (*Confederación Regional de Obreros Mexicanos*)

CRT   Revolutionary Confederation of Workers (*Confederación Revolucionaria de Trabajadores*)

CSUM   Unitary Syndical Confederation of Mexico (*Confederación Sindical Unitaria de México*)

CT   Congress of Labor (*Congreso del Trabajo*)

CTC   Confederation of Workers and Peasants (*Confederación de Trabajadores y Campesinos*)

CTM   Confederation of Mexican Workers (*Confederación de Trabajadores de México*)

CUT	Unified Central Body of Workers (*Central Unica de Trabajadores*)
FAO	Federation of Workers' Organizations (*Federación de Agrupaciones Obreros*)
FAT	Authentic Front of Labor (*Frente Auténtico de Trabajo*)
FCP	Communist Federation of the National Proletariat (*Federación Comunista del Proletarido*)
FNAP	National Popular Action Front (*Frente Nacional de Acción Popular*)
FNSI	National Federation of Independent Unions (*Federación Nacional de Sindicatos Independentes*)
FONACOT	National Fund for the Development and Guarantee of Workers' Consumption (*Fondo Nacional de Fomento y Garantía de Consumo para los Trabajadores*)
FSTDF	Syndicalist Federation of Workers of the Federal District (*Federación Sindical de Trabajadores del Distrito Federal*)
FSTSE	Federation of Unions of Workers in the Service of the State (*Federación de Sindicatos de Trabajadores al Servicio del Estado*)
FTDF	Federation of Federal District Workers (*Federación de Trabajadores del Distrito Federal*)
FTG	Federation of Guerrero Workers (*Federación de Trabajadores de Guerrero*)
FTN	Nayarit Workers' Federation (*Federación de Trabajadores de Nayarit*)
GCATRM	Large Confederation of Associations of Workers of the Mexican Republic (*Gran Confederación de Asociaciones de Trabajadores de la República Mexicana para los Trabajadores*)
IMSS	The Mexican Institute of Social Security (*Instituto Mexicano de Seguridad Social*)
INFONAVIT	Workers' Housing Institute (*Instituto Nacional del Fondo Nacional de la Vivienda para los Trabajadores*)

ISSSTE	Security and Social Services Institute for Government Workers (*Instituto de Seguridad y Servicios Sociales para Trabajdores de Estado*)
MCS	Table of Trade Union Harmony (*Mesa de Concertación Sindical*)
PAN	National Action Party (*Partido de Acción Nacional*)
Pemex	Mexican State Oil Company (*Petróleos Mexicanos*)
PLM	Mexican Labor Party (*Partido Laborista Mexicano*)
PLM	Mexican Liberal Party (*Partido Liberal Mexicano*)
PMS	Mexican Socialist Party (*Partido Mexicano de Socialismo*)
PNR	National Revolutionary Party (*Partido Nacional Revolucionario*)
PP	The Popular Party (*Partido Popular*)
PRD	Party of the Democratic Revolution (*Partido de la Revolución Democrática*)
PRI	Institutional Revolutionary Party (*Partido Revolucionario Institucional*)
PRM	Party of the Mexican Revolution (*Partido de la Revolución Mexicana*)
PRT	Revolutionary Workers' Party (*Partido Revolucionario de Trabajadores*)
PSE	Economic Solidarity Pact (*Pacto de Solidaridad Económica*)
PSUM	Unified Mexican Socialist Party (*Partido Socialista Unificado de México*)
SITMMSRM	Industrial Union of Miners, Metallurgical Workers and Allied Trades of the Mexican Republic (*Sindicato Industrial de Trabajadores Mineros, Metalúrgicos y Similares de la República Mexicana*)
SITUAR-100	Union of minibus drivers
SME	Mexican Electricians' Union (*Sindicato Mexicano de Electricistas*)

SNE	National Electricians' Union (*Sindicato Nacional de Electricistas*)
SNTE	National Union of Educational Workers (*Sindicato Nacional de Trabajadores de la Educación*)
SNTEISSSTE	Union of Employees of the Social Security Agency for State Workers (*Sindicato Nacional de Trabajadores y Empleados de la ISSSTE*)
SNTSSA	National Union of Workers of the Secretariat of Health and Welfare (*Sindicato Nacional de Trabajadores de la Secretaría de Salubridad y Asistencia*)
SRTPRM	Oil Workers' Union (*Sindicato Revolucionario de Trabajadores Petroleros de la Revolución Mexicana*)
STCRSRM	Union of Garment Workers and Allied Trades of the Mexican Republic (*Sindicato de Trabajadores de Confección de Ropa y Similares de la República Mexicana*)
STERM	Electrical Workers' Union (*Sindicato de Trabajadores Electricistas de la República Mexicana*)
STFRM	Union of Railroad Workers of the Mexican Republic (*Sindicato de Trabajadores Ferrocarrileros de la República Mexicana*)
STRM	Union of Telephone Workers of the Mexican Republic (*Sindicato de Telefonistas de la República Mexicana*)
STSTC	Union of Collective Transport Workers (*Sindicato de Trabajadores del Sistema de Transporte Colectivo*)
STUNAM	Union of Workers at the National Autonomous University of Mexico (*Sindicato de Trabajadores de la Universidad Nacional Autónoma de México*)
SUNTU	Single National Union of University Workers (*Sindicato Unico Nacional de Trabajadores Universitarios*)

SUTERM	Single Union of Electrical Workers of the Mexican Republic (*Sindicato Unico de Trabajadores Electricistas de la República Mexicana*)
SUTIN	Single Union of Workers of the Nuclear Industry (*Sindicato Unico de Trabajadores de la Industria Nuclear*)
UGOCM	General Union of Workers and Peasants of Mexico (*Unión General de Obreros y Campesinos de México*)
UOI/MPI	United Independent Workers/International Proletarian Movement (*Unidad Obrero Independiente/ Movimento Proleratario Internacional*)
UNAM	National Autonomous University of Mexico (*La Universidad Nacional Autónoma de México*)
USTIL	Syndical Union of Dairy Industry Workers (*Unión Sindical de Trabajadores de la Industria Lechera*)